# MYSTERIES
*of the*
# ANCIENT
# WORLD

# MYSTERIES *of the*

by *Toni Eugene*

# ANCIENT WORLD

NATIONAL GEOGRAPHIC

WASHINGTON , D. C.

# Contents

## Foreword

BY GEORGE STUART

6

## Chapter 1

SILENT STONES OF EUROPE:
STONEHENGE

12

## Chapter 2

THE MOUND BUILDERS:
PIONEERS OF ANCIENT AMERICA

48

## Chapter 3

STANDING SOLDIERS OF THE TIGER OF QIN:
MOUNT LI

70

# Chapter 4

## PUZZLE OF THE PAMPA:
## PERU'S NASCA LINES

### 92

# Chapter 5

## SENTINELS OF RAPA NUI:
## EASTER ISLAND

### 128

# Chapter 6

## AFRICA'S CITY OF STONE:
## GREAT ZIMBABWE

### 164

ADDITIONAL READING 186

INDEX 187

PAGE 1: TERRA-COTTA FIGURE EXCAVATED IN 1998 NEAR THE
TOMB OF QIN SHI HUANG DI MAY BE ONE OF CHINA'S EARLIEST
REALISTIC LIFE-SIZE STATUES.
PAGES 2-3: STONES RING AN ANCIENT SITE IN THE BLEAK HEIGHTS
OF DARTMOOR, IN SOUTHERN ENGLAND, ONE OF SOME 600 STONE
CIRCLES IN THE BRITISH ISLES.

# Foreword

FOR ME, ARCHAEOLOGY HAS BEEN A HIGHLY REWARDING CAREER, FOR I AM interested both in people and in the past. I also like a good challenge. In seeking to know ancient cultures, we have to rely on ridiculously small samples of remains that have survived, from artifacts of stone, pottery, or other durable materials to the traces of ancient writing systems requiring decipherment. From these we attempt to reconstruct the past lives of individuals or of entire peoples and civilizations, to note the changes that took place among past cultures, and to explain how and why and when such changes took place. The most difficult—some would say impossible—obstacle we archaeologists face is studying other peoples across the vast chasm of time and culture that separates us.

Re-creating ancient lives from the scant evidence available inevitably creates mysteries—known achievements or events of the past that defy explanation: How did the ancient Egyptians build the pyramids? What caused the apparent collapse of the glorious civilization of the Classic Maya?

Efforts to solve such mysteries often create purely speculative explanations by all manner of people seeking answers. Such solutions have involved, among other things, incredibly talented aliens from outer space, the precocious civilization of sunken Atlantis, and other things that can never be proved. For most of us archaeologists and other rationally minded people, these explanations do not answer many questions.

This book looks at some of the great archaeological mysteries of the ancient world and how archaeologists and their colleagues have solved many of them—at least partially. Its geographical range touches six out of the seven inhabited continents. In terms of time, its chapters use the term "ancient" with its customary looseness, as having a slightly different definition depending on the area. The mysteries addressed here range in date from as early as 2000 B.C. to as late as A.D. 1650.

The Great Pyramid of Giza looms as perhaps the best known symbol of archaeological mystery. It stands with its smaller companion pyramids and the famously enigmatic Sphinx in the northern valley of Egypt's Nile River. A tangible, and therefore measurable, structure, this awesome pile of carefully laid gigantic stones—the largest pyramid ever built—has become many things to many awed observers, an embodiment of numerological formulas that provide a key to life, a powerful source of energy, a marker for those observing Earth from outer space—or all of the above.

For Egyptologists, the evidence of archaeology and the historical texts show the Great Pyramid as the tomb of the all-powerful Khufu, Pharaoh of the 4th dynasty (circa 2600-2500 B.C.). As for its construction, the best arguments favor the transport of the huge blocks of stone from the quarries to Giza by sheer human force—work gangs aided by special sledges with runners. How were the blocks raised? Probably by the construction of ramps of rocks and sand, some of a volume so great that they may have exceeded the finished structure itself. However it was built, the nearly perfectly square base of the enormous structure covers more than 13 acres, and this base, even after 4,500 years, is but one inch out of level!

These data on the construction of the Great Pyramid do not mean that all mystery has been stripped from this extraordinary structure—quite the contrary. As modern technology improves, so do the tools available to the archaeologist. Now there are sonic and other invisible probes that allow us to search for new passages or cavities inside. One such probe, a robot sent into an ancient air shaft in the Great Pyramid, was stopped about 200 feet in by what appeared to be a stone door with two copper handles. It is unlikely that the aura of mystery that attends this unique construction will ever disperse completely. I hope not.

North across the Mediterranean from the Nile Delta lay another puzzling ruin—the Palace of Minos at Knossos, Crete. Its elaborate architectural plan likely provided the ancient Greeks with an apt setting for their legend of the labyrinth and the terrifying minotaur, half man, half bull, that lurked in its dark passages. Decades of excavation of the palace have revealed not only the extraordinarily complicated floor plan that inspired the legend but also the history of the palace in the context of the Mediterranean world of the second millennium B.C. The Minoans, builders of the palace at Knossos and others on Crete, began their work around 2000 B.C. By 1700 B.C., the entire island served as the seat of the powerful kings and sea traders of Minoan civilization, whose power endured until natural forces—earthquakes and volcanic eruptions—and cultural forces—the might of its Mycenaean neighbors—ended Minoan power some 250 years later.

In 1908, in the ruins of the Minoan palace at Phaistos, Crete, archaeologists discovered a small clay disk bearing mysterious inscriptions on both sides. The puzzling piece contains 45 different glyphs, symbols pressed into the clay, in two long sequences containing a total of 261, with the inscription on each side meticulously arranged in a spiral. For nearly a century, the Phaistos Disk has gained fame as one of the great mysteries of antiquity. Unlike specimens of other

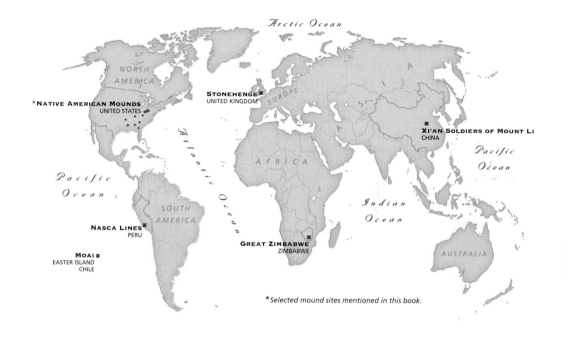

Arctic Ocean

NORTH AMERICA

EUROPE

ASIA

*NATIVE AMERICAN MOUNDS
UNITED STATES

STONEHENGE■
UNITED KINGDOM

XI'AN SOLDIERS OF MOUNT LI
CHINA

Pacific Ocean

Pacific Ocean

Atlantic Ocean

AFRICA

Indian Ocean

NASCA LINES■
PERU

SOUTH AMERICA

GREAT ZIMBABWE
ZIMBABWE

AUSTRALIA

MOAI■
EASTER ISLAND
CHILE

*Selected mound sites mentioned in this book.

**ARCHAEOLOGICAL SITES AROUND THE GLOBE HAVE LURED LAYMEN AS WELL AS SCIENTISTS FOR CENTURIES. EXPERTS HAVE SOLVED MANY MYSTERIES, BUT SIX SPOTS REMAIN PARTICULARLY INTRIGUING.**

writing systems used in the eastern Mediterranean at the time, the writing on the disk—if indeed that's what it is—has defied satisfactory decipherment. Many have claimed success, however, calling the Phaistos inscription a prayer, a legal document, a farming almanac, the story of humanity, an energy chart, the proof of a geometric theorem, and a call to arms, to name only a few of its interpretations. The range of these readings is not surprising, for in theory any unique, relatively short "text" of this sort has an infinite number of solutions, of which many might actually make sense. But as long as there are no other examples of the same script to act as a test for decipherment, the mystery must remain.

In contrast, the successful and now largely accepted decipherment of the ancient Maya writing system used in southeast Mexico and neighboring parts of Central

America for about the first 1,500 years A.D. has solved a longstanding mystery. Today the ancient Maya script—a mixed system of words and syllables that essentially spell words—is almost totally readable. Working simultaneously on the writing and the ruins, students of ancient Maya culture continue to reveal a world that prospered between around A.D. 250 and A.D. 900 and over a territory about half the size of Texas, with dozens of regional states centered on great cities such as Tikal, Copan, Palenque, and Caracol. In each of these capitals and in many, many others, a society of farmers, merchants, artisans, architects, and priests lived, ruled by kings or queens of noble and divine descent.

The deciphered texts tell the names of some of the great rulers of American antiquity, such as Pakal of Palenque. They offer the stories of wars waged among the Maya cities and states, the dates and rites accompanying the dedications of temples, and the signatures of their scribes and sculptors. Other texts deal with mythical history and the births of the gods in distant time.

One thing the texts don't reveal is the cause of the sudden decline of Tikal and the other great cities in the Maya heartland around A.D. 900. This so-called Maya collapse remains perhaps this culture's greatest mystery of all. People working on the problem cite climate change, overpopulation, warfare, deforestation, and other factors as possible causes of the collapse. Perhaps all of them are right. Whatever the final conclusions, the puzzle of the Maya collapse reminds us that the solving of any mystery of the ancient past, large or small, may well hold valuable, even essential, lessons for our own world.

The chapters ahead speak of archaeological mysteries from Stonehenge to Great Zimbabwe and from the Americas to Asia and Oceania—and reveal how investigators, even as they solve these mysteries, uncover new puzzles about our past.

*— George Stuart, Barnardsville, North Carolina, 2004*

CELEBRANTS THRONG STONEHENGE AT THE SUMMER SOLSTICE.
ON JUNE 21, 2003, MORE THAN 30,000 PEOPLE GATHERED TO GREET THE
SUNRISE AT THE HUGE RING OF MEGALITHS IN WILTSHIRE, ENGLAND.

# Silent Stones of Europe

## STONEHENGE

# Chapter One

**AN UNADORNED STONE MONUMENT**
on the chalky plains of southern England, Stonehenge has inspired legends, lore, and scholarly curiosity for more than 800 years. Who built it? Why? How? Archaeologists still search for answers they may never find. Stonehenge's location is ordinary—an empty grassland west of London. It is a simple structure: Just 162 stones enclose a circle 35 paces across. Yet, as the sun rises over its Heel Stone at the midsummer solstice, and as the sun sinks between the uprights of the great megalith at its center at the mid-winter solstice, an aura of mystery and magic envelops the 5,000-year-old site. The Stonehenge that rises from the Salisbury Plain today evolved over a period of more than 1,500 years. Ancient agrarians who raised cattle, sheep, and grew cereal grains in the Wessex grasslands built the monument over 60 to 70 generations. Its name, combining the Saxon words "stone" and "henge," once meant "place of

the hanging stones," a reference to the famous uprights topped with lintels that characterize the circle. The most famous, perhaps the most mysterious, and certainly the most elaborate and carefully crafted, Stonehenge is only one of more than 600 prehistoric stone circles in the British Isles.

Thousands of huge stone monuments known as megaliths are scattered throughout Ireland, Great Britain, and western Europe. The oldest, Stonehenge among them, date from the Neolithic Age, beginning about 4500 B.C. The most recent were constructed some 3,000 years later, in the Bronze Age. At the time of the summer and winter solstices, many of these monuments align with the rising or setting sun. Some, like Stonehenge, and Scotland's Standing Stones of Callanish, may have served as astronomical observatories. Some, like Newgrange, in eastern Ireland, were tombs. Others, like Avebury, north of Stonehenge, were ritual sites.

AVEBURY IS A HENGE, SO CALLED BECAUSE, LIKE STONEHENGE, IT IS A MORE OR LESS circular area bounded by a bank of material dug from a quarry, usually on the inside of the ring. A henge has an entrance, or two at opposite sides, marked by a causeway. At Avebury, for example, a double line of upright stones leads almost a mile to the ring-shaped embankment. A village lies now within the 1,380-foot diameter of the earthen ring. A ditch on the inside of the ring, created when the bank was built, encloses an area of some 28 acres. The bank, now 30 feet high, reached 50 feet, measuring from the bottom of the ditch, when the henge was completed, before 2000 B.C. Then some 98 stones lined the inside of the circle, the largest weighing more than 60 tons. Within that great circle rose two additional rings of standing stones, each more than 300 feet across.

Only remnants of the three circles of upright stones remain, the largest of the stones today 19 feet tall. Many were broken up during the Middle Ages, when villagers believed the megalith might have been the work of the devil. Avebury is still an enigma; archaeologists can agree only that the complex was most likely a religious or ritual center. Even the significance of its circular shape eludes the experts.

White quartz faces the huge mound at Ireland's Newgrange. A man-made tunnel leads 60 feet into a beehive-shaped chamber lavishly decorated with geometric patterns. Smaller rooms set into the walls hold saucerlike stone basins about four

AN EMBANKMENT OF GRASS-COVERED CHALK STONE 1,380 FEET IN DIAMETER RINGS
THE WILTSHIRE VILLAGE OF AVEBURY, 20 MILES NORTH OF STONEHENGE.
SOME HUNDRED STONES ONCE CIRCLED THE HENGE; 27 STILL STAND.

feet wide, which may have once held bones. On the shortest day of the year, the midwinter solstice, the rising sun beams light down the long passageway and shines on the farthest wall of the chamber. In addition to its role as a tomb, Newgrange may have been a ceremonial center that hosted an annual event of great import.

Some 150 tombs with huge, slanting capstones dot the Irish countryside. Experts surmise that ancient people buried their revered dead in such spots as Poulnabrone, in the Burren of County Clare, but why and how they moved stones weighing as much as one hundred tons to create these sites remain a mystery.

Maeshowe, perhaps the finest example of an ancient tomb in all of Great Britain, lies in the Orkney Islands of northern Scotland. A passage of layered stone leads 8 feet from the 4$^1$/$_2$-foot-high doorway to another 16-foot aisle of walls, with a roof crafted of huge stone slabs. Large chunks of sandstone extend the entire length of the tomb's walls; save the one with the passage door, each contains a chamber 5 feet

MYSTERIES OF THE ANCIENT WORLD

LOW CLOUDS VEIL A STANDING STONE OF THE RING OF BROGAR
IN THE ORKNEY ISLANDS OF NORTHERN SCOTLAND. OF AN ESTIMATED 60 ERECTED,
27 REMAIN. THE RING'S TALLEST MEGALITH RISES 15 FEET.

across and 3 feet high, roofed with a single stone slab. The largest of these stones weighs more than three tons. Some of the joints fit so closely that the blade of a knife will not slide into them.

The Ring of Brogar, another of Orkney's megalithic treasures, lies on a neck of land between two lakes. Inside a circular ditch 370 feet in diameter rise 27 stones, their flat sides facing inward. They are the remains of an estimated 60 stones that originally graced the ring. The tallest of the standing stones rises 15 feet above the ground. Alexander Thom, a Scottish professor of engineering at Oxford University, advanced a theory to explain the existence of the Ring of Brogar. In the 1930s Thom began making careful surveys of the stone circles throughout Great Britain. In 1971 and 1972 he surveyed the Ring of Brogar and concluded that it was a sophisticated lunar observatory.

By standing in the center of the ring, Thom noted, an ancient astronomer could have seen four natural landmarks on the horizon. Thom determined that the landmarks, which he called "foresights," aligned with the positions where the moon rose or set on important dates through a cycle of 18.6 years.

The easiest Brogar foresight to see today is the slope of a high cliff some five miles southwest of the ring. The moon seems to slide down the cliff as it sets on one of the significant dates. Starting near the ring, a line of mounds or cairns—man-made rockpiles—points toward each landmark. By sighting down the lines, ancient astronomers could have studied the small irregularities in the moon's movements caused by the pull of the sun's gravity. Over generations of observations, the astronomers would have noted cycles in the moon's course that would have helped them predict lunar eclipses.

A group of megaliths on the Isle of Lewis, in the Outer Hebrides of Scotland, inspired Thom's studies. Called the Standing Stones of Callanish, they form a cross more than 400 feet long. In the center, 13 tall stones ring a megalith that towers nearly 16 feet above the remains of a small grave. Thom noted that the North Star shone directly in line with the north-south row of stones. By sighting along one of the short arms of the cross, an astronomer would have seen where the sun rose at the vernal and autumnal equinoxes, the two days of the year when day and night are the same length.

Alexander Thom took thousands of measurements at European megalithic sites, and his are generally still considered the most accurate ever made. Based on those measurements, he drew three conclusions. Many sites aligned with prominent features on the horizon, allowing ancient astronomers to make precise observations of the movements of the sun and moon. Many of the rings, Thom noted, were not strictly circular. They were, rather, variations constructed through the application

CAREFUL CRANE WORK RESTORES A STONEHENGE LINTEL THAT TOPPLED IN 1797.

IN THE 1950S RICHARD ATKINSON, STUART PIGGOTT, AND JOHN STONE DIRECTED

A MAJOR RESTORATION AND EXCAVATIONS AT THE ANCIENT SITE.

of sophisticated geometry. Finally, Thom stated, the builders of the stone circles used a common unit of measurement exactly 2.72 feet long. Thom christened that distance the "megalithic yard."

Thom's reports inspired controversy among mathematicians, astronomers, and archaeologists. Most scholars accepted the accuracy of his measurements, but many disagreed with his hypotheses. The argument still rages. Thom, insist his detractors, assumed too much. Just because modern mathematicians can use the circles for calculations, that is no proof that the people who erected them did so. We can reproduce the shapes of sites using geometry, but that does not prove that the builders did. Finally, Thom's concept of the megalithic yard implies coordination and communication among widely separated groups thousands of years ago.

Across the English Channel, hundreds of miles from Stonehenge, Thom measured and surveyed megalithic sites near Carnac, in Brittany, France. Four huge stones, the broken pieces of a site called the Grand Menhir Brisé, lie on the Locmariaquer Peninsula. When whole, the menhir—a Breton word for monolith— would have been 65 to 70 feet high. Thom thought it once served as a foresight to observe the moon's movements.

At the village of Le Menec, arrow-straight avenues of stones, some 2,500 of them, march in parallel rows miles long. Thom, the first scholar to study them carefully, suggested that the stone rows served as a computing grid. They were, he believed, a kind of stone graph to aid in working out the complex mathematics involved in calculating lunar movements. This conclusion, too, is still the subject of debate.

THE STONEHENGE THAT RISES TODAY FROM THE CHALK PLAINS OF SALISBURY contains horseshoe and rectangular shapes rare in other megalithic sites in Britain and Ireland. British archaeologist Aubrey Burl has studied the circles for more than three decades. In his book, *Great Stone Circles,* Burl notes that Stonehenge was constructed in the Breton style and is more similar to sites near Brittany's Carnac than to other British sites. Stonehenge, he concludes, may have been built by Bretons who invaded Wessex.

Of the hundreds of megaliths scattered across Great Britain and Brittany, Stonehenge is the most prominent and the most popular. It is located about 80 miles west of London on a chalky plain in south-central England. Dry, stunted grasses cradle the huge old stones at the top of a gentle slope in rolling downlands. Stonehenge rises in the center of a circular enclosure bounded by a ditch; a break in the northeastern corner forms a causeway 35 feet wide leading into and out of the circle. The exterior structure of Stonehenge—the most famous and the most familiar—is called the sarsen circle. Its uprights and lintels are composed of sarsen, a durable sandstone. These stones were quarried in the Avebury region, some 20 miles north. Thirty uprights stand in a circle about a hundred feet in diameter; each rises about $13^1/_2$ feet above the plain. The uprights support horizontal lintels, each some $2^3/_4$ feet thick and $10^1/_2$ feet long. Some lintels are missing, but the uprights form a continuous circle of stone.

AT TWILIGHT SHEEP CLAIM THE GRASS INSIDE THE STANDING STONES OF STENNES,
BUILT ON THE MAIN ISLAND OF SCOTLAND'S ORKNEYS IN THE THIRD MILLENNIUM B.C.

Immediately inside the sarsen circle rises a ring of smaller, bluish igneous rocks. This bluestone circle is less regular than the sarsen and about 75 feet in diameter. The stones, about $6^1/_2$ feet high, hold no lintels. Only six of them still remain upright; the rest lean, lie flat, or have broken into fragments. Unlike the sarsens, quarried locally, the bluestones originated in the Preseli Mountains

MENHIRS—SINGLE STANDING STONES—CROWD A MEADOW IN CARNAC, FRANCE
(ABOVE). THE VILLAGE IN BRITTANY BRISTLES WITH SOME 3,000 STONE MONUMENTS.
AMONG THEM LOOM MANY DOLMENS, MEGALITHIC TOMBS OF STONE (BELOW).

of southwestern Wales, about 240 miles due west of the Salisbury Plain. How they were transported to the plain is another of the many mysteries that the site of Stonehenge presents.

Inside the bluestone circle stand five more sarsen structures, each a horizontal lintel set on two stone uprights. These structures are called trilithons, from the Greek meaning "three stones." The uprights, set close together, form a symmetrical horseshoe shape about 45 feet across. The lintels are not continuous. The size of the trilithons varies; the smallest are 20 feet high. Of the great trilithon, only one upright now stands, rising 22 feet above the ground, one of the tallest ancient stones still erect in the British Isles. The stone lintels found in the sarsen circle and horseshoe are unique to Stonehenge. Furthermore, these stones have been trimmed, another feature that distinguishes Stonehenge from other British stone circles.

Just as a smaller bluestone circle rises within the great sarsen circle, a horseshoe of upright bluestones without lintels lies within the sarsen horseshoe. Six of its pillars, square in section, are still in place, the shortest less than six feet tall. Like the sarsen trilithons, the bluestones increase in size to the southwest.

The fifth component of the Stonehenge complex is known as the Altar Stone. A single slab of greenish-gray sandstone, it lies on the ground toward the rear of the inner horseshoe, largely hidden between fallen chunks of the great trilithon. This 16-foot-long slab, whose name may give hints as to its original purpose, probably once stood upright.

A bank has formed on the inside of the ditch that rings Stonehenge, created when the site was excavated and chalk dug out. That bank is now heavily eroded. Two sarsen blocks, the Station Stones, lie just inside the bank, one to the northwest and the other to the southeast. Small ditches mark the sites where two other station stones once opposed them.

On the east side of the causeway, flat in the dirt formed by a break in the bank and ditch, sprawls the Slaughter Stone. Eighteenth-century admirers gave the 21- by 7-foot slab its name, since its humps, runnels, and hollows seemed suited to catch the blood of sacrificial victims. Some 85 feet outside the causeway lies the Heel Stone, a title bestowed by an observer one century earlier who described "a cavity something resembling the print of a man's foot." A single untrimmed sarsen, the Heel Stone is almost 16 feet tall. This rough, lichen-encrusted boulder dates from the earliest building period at Stonehenge, which began nearly 5,000 years ago.

ARCHAEOLOGISTS AGREE THAT STONEHENGE WAS BUILT IN STAGES. Evidence indicates that by 4000 B.C., farming communities were prevalent in the

MYSTERIES OF THE ANCIENT WORLD

IN THE GRASSLANDS OF THE ORKNEY ISLANDS, SCOTLAND'S RING OF BROGAR

RISES INSIDE A DITCH 370 FEET IN DIAMETER. OF THE STONE CIRCLE'S

60 ORIGINAL MASSIVE MENHIRS, 27 REMAIN STANDING.

area. Farmers on the Salisbury Plain built elongated mounds that often contained remains of the dead. These mounds may have served as territorial markers. The area contains one of the densest concentrations of prehistoric sites in Europe. Settlements and ceremonial centers are so diverse and numerous near Stonehenge that they bear testament to the great symbolic significance of this southern English landscape. Barrows, or mounds, for collective burials predate even the first stage of Stonehenge's construction. When the site was chosen for building, it already supported a complex of ceremonial structures several centuries old.

Old Stonehenge was one of five henges in the region. During the first phase of its construction, about 3000 B.C., ancient Britons dug the original ditch, a simple circle, with picks made of deer antlers. They piled up the chalk from the excavation to make a six-foot bank. They left a broad entranceway, today's causeway, on the northeast side of the circle.

One set of features dating back to Stonehenge's earliest times is known as the Aubrey Holes, named after the 17th-century author John Aubrey, who was fascinated with Stonehenge and Avebury. Aubrey marked 56 slight cavities spaced about every 16 feet within the bank. These roughly circular pits seem to have held standing stones or posts. Some also held cremated bones, but their true purpose is unknown. The holes were filled soon after they were dug. Round concrete markers on the eastern side of the circle are the only remnants of their existence.

Inhabitants of the area used the first Stonehenge for several centuries, then abandoned it long before any sarsens or bluestones were erected. Stonehenge served during that time as a relatively unimportant mortuary site. Meanwhile, other imposing ceremonial monuments were being built nearby, such as a huge earthen mound at Silbury Hill near Avebury. In sharp contrast to Stonehenge—where, as if to restrict access to the site, the encircling bank was erected on the inside of the ditch—in these other henges, the ditch lay inside the encircling bank, enclosing circular settings of timber or stones.

The first remodeling of Stonehenge began about 2150 B.C., the period of the monument's greatest glory. Changes and reconstruction were constant. The axis of Stonehenge was shifted slightly to the east, thus aligning the entrance with the rising sun at the midsummer solstice. The changed orientation seems to have been deliberate, inspired by a religious purpose. Builders began construction of a ceremonial avenue that faced the new entrance. A pair of parallel banks and ditches, the avenue ran cross-country for about 500 yards from the new entrance.

Archaeologists have not determined when the Station Stones were erected. Originally, four small sarsens were set up just inside the bank, forming a rectangle.

BROKEN BONES UNEARTHED THREE MILES FROM STONEHENGE IN 2002
INTRIGUED ARCHAEOLOGISTS. ANALYSIS INDICATED A RELATIONSHIP, PERHAPS SON
AND FATHER, BETWEEN THIS SKELETON AND ANOTHER FOUND NEARBY. BOTH GRAVES
HELD GOLD HAIR TRESSES, INDICATING THE STATUS AND POWER OF THE MEN.

Of those four, only two remain. They intersect the Aubrey Holes, implying that they were erected after the early stage of construction. One of them is largely unshaped and thus might belong to an early phase, while the other is well trimmed, like the great sarsens erected later.

THE GREATEST PERIOD OF BUILDING ACTIVITY AT STONEHENGE OCCURRED between 2100 and 2000 B.C. Workers dragged ten great sarsen stones some 20 miles southwest from the Marlborough Downs. Stoneworkers trimmed, smoothed, and shaped slabs that weighed up to 25 tons, some even more. Those ten sarsens were set up in a horseshoe shape, becoming the uprights for the lintels that would complete the five trilithons. Then 30 smaller uprights were set up, shaping an outer circle, and 30 lintels were placed on top of them to form a continuous circle.

No other stone circle in Britain has lintels on top of uprights. In this design, Stonehenge was unique. It was different, too, in its incorporation of carpentry techniques to hold the lintels to the uprights. Large stones were rare on the Salisbury Plain, but wood was plentiful, so techniques for its use had been developed. It seems that the builders of Stonehenge relied on skills they already possessed to build their monument. They shaped conical tenons, or pegs, on the tops of the uprights that fit into mortises, or pits, hollowed into the lintels—a classic technique for joining wood timbers. The lintels that covered the uprights to form the trilithons of the outer circle were held together with tongue-and-groove shaping.

Experts still disagree on many details of Stonehenge's construction, including exactly how the builders moved and erected the great stones. While they are rare on the Salisbury Plain, sarsens littered the slopes of the Marlborough Downs, and experts agree it was the source of the stones. Some suggest that the slabs, which averaged 25 tons each, were moved cross-country on rollers; others suggest that rafts carried the huge stones south on the Avon River.

Most probably, when the sarsens arrived at Stonehenge, stonemasons worked for weeks to taper the slabs. They used mauls—wooden-headed hammers—and turned the stones with large wooden levers to shape all sides. Then they pounded the surfaces to smooth them. Meanwhile, villagers dug a circle of deep, ramped holes to hold the huge uprights. A team rolled the sarsen slab to its pit, then used massive

PAINSTAKINGLY RESTORED, A VESSEL FROM A MASS GRAVE FOUND IN WILTSHIRE IN 2003 TYPIFIES THE SHAPE THAT GAVE ITS NAME TO A GROUP OF PREHISTORIC INHABITANTS OF SOUTHERN BRITAIN: THE BEAKER PEOPLE. THE GRAVE'S EIGHT BEAKERS ONCE HELD FOOD AND DRINK FOR THE JOURNEY TO THE NEXT LIFE.

BLINDFOLDED INITIATES PROCESS BY HUNDREDS OF BROTHERS TO TAKE THE OATH
OF THE ANCIENT ORDER OF DRUIDS AT STONEHENGE ON AUGUST 24, 1905.
ALTHOUGH THE MODERN SECRET SOCIETY WAS FOUNDED IN 1781,
STONEHENGE HAS BEEN ASSOCIATED WITH ANCIENT CELTIC DRUIDS SINCE 1666,
THANKS TO WILTSHIREMAN AND HISTORIAN JOHN AUBREY.

From Golgonooza the spiritual Four fold London eternal
In immense labours & sorrows, ever building, ever rolling
Thro Albions four Forests which overspread all the Earth.
From London Stone to Blackheath east: to Hounslow west:
To Finchley north: to Norwood south: and the weights
Of Enitharmons Loom play lulling cadences on the
        winds of Albion
From Caithness in the north, to Lizard-point & Dover in the south

Loud sounds the Hammer of Los, & loud his Bellows is heard
Before London to Hampsteads breadths & Highgates heights To
Stratford & old Bow: & across to the Gardens of Kensington
On Tyburns Brook: loud groans Thames beneath the iron Forge
Of Rintrah & Palamabron of Theotorm & Bromion. to
        forge the instruments
Of Harvest: the Plow & Harrow to pass over the Nations

The Surrey hills glow like the clinkers of the furnace: Lambeths Vale
Where Jerusalems foundations began: where they were laid in ruins
Where they were laid in ruins from every Nation & Oak Groves rooted
Dark gleams before the Furnace-mouth a heap of burning ashes
When shall Jerusalem return & overspread all the Nations
Return: return to Lambeths Vale O building of human souls
Thence stony Druid Temples overspread the Island white
And thence from Jerusalems ruins, from her walls of salvation
And praise: thro the whole Earth were reard from Ireland
To Mexico & Peru west, & east to China & Japan: till Babel
The Spectre of Albion frownd over the Nations in glory & war
All things begin & end in Albions ancient Druid rocky shore
But now the Starry Heavens are fled
        from the mighty limbs of
                Albion

                                        armed

Loud sounds the Hammer of Los, loud turn the Wheels of Enith-
Her Looms vibrate with soft affections, weaving the Web of Life
Out from the ashes of the Dead; Los lifts his iron Ladles
With molten ore: he heaves the iron cliffs in his rattling chains
From Hyde Park to the Alms-houses of Mile-end & old Bow
Here the Three Classes of Mortal Men take their fixd destinations
And hence they overspread the Nations of the whole Earth & hence
The Web of Life is woven: & the tender sinews of life created
And the Three Classes of Men regulated by Los's Hammer, and
                                        woven

timbers to lever it down the ramp and into its foundation. To hold the heavy stones steady, the holes had to be deep. The great 22-foot trilithon had to be sunk 8 feet into the chalky subsurface to sustain its height and weight against the tug of gravity.

To raise the stones, workers most likely inserted timbers under an upright until it was angled above the ground, then yanked the stone upward at the same time that other villagers rushed to pack stones and soil around the base. For each lintel, workers built a wooden platform underneath around the two uprights on which they intended it to rest. Then they inserted timbers underneath the lintel stone, slowly raising it until it was level with the uprights. While it rested on the platform, masons shaped the mortise holes, then turned the stone over and levered it into place over the round tenons already carved in the uprights.

The creation of the sarsen circle took years; we will probably never know how many. Nor do we know if the lintel ring, now incomplete, was once finished. One sarsen is thinner and narrower than its 29 mates—perhaps the builders were running out of stones. Or, as amateur astronomer Peter Newham postulated in the 1960s, maybe the smaller stone was a deliberate attempt to have the uprights of the outer circle represent the lunar month of $29^1/_2$ days. These are among the many mysteries of Stonehenge that archaeologists will probably never solve.

FROM ABOUT 2000 TO 1550 B.C., THE ANCIENT BRITONS CONTINUED TO MODIFY their monument. They erected an oval of 20 bluestones within the great sarsen circle. Experts agree that the bluestones were quarried in the Preseli Mountains of southwestern Wales, where tumbled piles of rocks like these are still evident. How these giant bluestones reached the Salisbury Plain is another of the many mysteries that still shroud Stonehenge.

Some 80 blocks comprise the inner horseshoe, and the stones weigh an average of four tons each. Moving them close to 240 miles from Wales to Wiltshire would demand almost superhuman effort. Yet many archaeologists believe that humans did move the slabs, transporting them overland to the coast, rafting them east along the shore and along rivers, then portaging them to Stonehenge. Aubrey Burl, the British archaeologist, considers such an accomplishment farfetched; he reasons that the blocks were glacial erratics that moved naturally, transported by prehistoric rivers of ice.

Not long after the bluestones were set up in a rough oval, they were reset into two groups: the bluestone horseshoe inside the sarsen horseshoe and the bluestone circle inside the sarsen circle. The Altar Stone, now fallen, stood on end at the apex of the horseshoe.

During the final phase of building, which began in about 1100 B.C., workers extended the avenue about a mile and a half to the Avon River. Finally, the temple was abandoned—when, we do not know, but it was probably around 1000 B.C., in the late Bronze Age. Archaeologists have determined a Roman presence at Stonehenge in post-Conquest times. In the first century, the Salisbury Plain stone circle may have sheltered Druids, although Stonehenge is atypical of the wooded and watery sites usually associated with that Celtic religion. Bronze coins from the fourth century A.D. found nearby imply that Stonehenge had by that time become a Roman tourist attraction.

But from then until the 11th century, Stonehenge stood unheralded and unremarked. In 1129 Henry, archdeacon of Huntingdon, termed it a wonder of Britain. He initiated the questions that many still seek to answer. Who built Stonehenge? What was its use? Surely the ancient Britons were incapable of such a project: Had Danes, Romans, Greeks, or even mythical giants built it?

In 1611 John Aubrey, who drew a rough plan of the site, asserted that Stonehenge was a Druid temple. Fifty years later, Dr. William Stukeley popularized that

ADMIRERS FROM AROUND THE WORLD POSE BEFORE THE STONEHENGE MEGALITHS.
INCREASED TOURISM, POLLUTION, AND ROAD BUILDING HAVE PROMPTED
ENGLISH HERITAGE, THE SITE'S CUSTODIAN, TO ANNOUNCE
A MULTI-MILLION-DOLLAR PLAN FOR A NEW VISITORS' CENTER.

idea. Stukeley was the first person to point out that the Stonehenge circle was oriented on the axis of the midsummer sun.

Stukeley's suggestion was the precursor to all later astronomical theories about Stonehenge. No one attempted a study of the ruins until 1740, when English architect John Wood drew the first accurate plan of the circle and its earthworks. Through the 19th century, though, prevailing scientific opinion still attributed Stonehenge to the Druids.

Tourists and visitors began to besiege the site. In 1918 local landholder Cecil Chubb donated Stonehenge to the British nation. The following year, the first large-scale excavations began. After World War II, archaeologists Stuart Piggott, Richard Atkinson, and John Stone, all of whom had vast experience unearthing sites in Wessex, began work at Stonehenge. In the 1950s Piggott, Atkinson, and Stone made suggestions as to how ancient Britons had transported, shaped, and erected the giant slabs at Stonehenge. They attempted to decipher the notes of their predecessors and applied a new tool—radiocarbon dating—to their meticulous excavations. Based on analysis of organic material at Stonehenge and other megaliths, they concluded that Stonehenge dated to about 2800 B.C. and had evolved over centuries.

Up until the early 1970s, archaeologists thought that Stonehenge and other megaliths were the product of the gradual westward spread of civilization from the Middle East. Daggers carved in the rocks of Stonehenge seemed to corroborate that theory: Their designs were similar in shape to those of daggers found in the ruins of Mycenae, in southern Greece. The revolution in radiocarbon dating, however, showed that many established dates, including those of the megaliths, were too recent.

In the study of ancient civilizations lying farther east, such as the Mycenaean culture, archaeologists could rely on written records, but not so in the study of Stonehenge and other European stone circles. The lack of written records related to such sites has meant that archaeologists have had to rely on radiocarbon dating. These techniques revealed that the megaliths were built before the eras represented by the civilizations once thought to be their source. New information dated Stonehenge to about 3000 B.C. and therefore indicated that the native inhabitants of western Europe were in fact the continent's first builders and architects in stone.

From the 1700s, when William Stukeley pinpointed its orientation on the axis of the midsummer sun, most experts had dismissed as ridiculous the idea that Stonehenge once served as an ancient observatory. Then, in the 1960s, amateur astronomer Peter Newham discovered the new alignments for the equinoxes and the moon that led him to hypothesize that the uprights of the outer circle, with one stone deliberately half the size of the other 29, represented the days of a lunar month. Soon after, British astronomer Gerald S. Hawkins offered insights into the central question of why Stonehenge was built.

Using a computer, Hawkins calculated the positions of the sun and moon over Stonehenge during the centuries of its construction. He concluded that the monument was an observatory used to study the cycles of the sun and moon. The 56 Aubrey Holes were used to predict eclipses of the moon. Of the 12 solar and lunar alignments he found, Hawkins determined a less-than-one-in-a-million chance that they would arise randomly.

Hawkins's findings met with skepticism at first, but gradually archaeologists began to accept many of them. Controversy continues, though, because he assumed that the alignments he found would be the same ones that the ancients used and because he relied exclusively on astronomy and failed to make use of available archaeological evidence.

AFTER CENTURIES OF STUDY, DISCUSSION, AND DESCRIPTION, STONEHENGE STILL abounds with mysteries. Why did Bronze Age farmers go to such great lengths to haul huge boulders long distances to an ordinary-looking chalk plain in the middle of downlands? Why did they spend centuries erecting and rearranging the slabs? Was Stonehenge the center of a long-forgotten religious cult? Was it an astronomical observatory, some sort of neolithic computer? Many henges incorporate wood or stone uprights; none except those at Stonehenge were transported from distant locations. No slabs elsewhere reflect the high quality of workmanship; none shows such architectural refinements as the mortar-and-tenon joints or the lintels of Stonehenge. What was so special and distinctive about this site?

Clearly this was a place of special power and influence, but archaeological evidence implies that Stonehenge was not an astronomical machine. It was a temple that may have reflected the cycles of the sun, moon, and stars across the sky, but little more. The ancient inhabitants of the Salisbury Plain were farmers. Without a doubt, Stonehenge helped them keep track of the passage of the seasons and helped them to determine the crucial times to reap and sow.

Surely, though, the monument was much more than that. Stonehenge and Europe's other great stone monuments continue to intrigue scientists and laymen, neighbors and travelers alike, who come great distances from around the world to stand in the presence of these stones and witness their grand and silent mysteries.

MYSTERIES OF THE ANCIENT WORLD

# MERLIN AND THE MEGALITH

The crafty magician Merlin has for many hundreds of years been identified with Good King Arthur and his mythical Eden called Camelot. Long before the fabled wizard became Arthur's mentor and personal sorcerer, however, Merlin entered English history books, identified as the person who had miraculously erected the stones of Stonehenge.

The massive stone complex on England's Salisbury Plain seems to have boggled the medieval mind as much as it does the modern one. Of the many theories and explanations for its existence offered over the centuries, one of the earliest was penned by the medieval chronicler Geoffrey of Monmouth. Also known as Galfridus Monemutensis, Geoffrey was an early historian whose work is considered an important source for stories about Arthur as well.

Born in Wales in about A.D. 1100, Geoffrey of Monmouth wrote his famous book, *Historia regum Britanniae—History of the Kings of Britain*—from 1136 to 1138. The tome was a pseudo history of the Britons—the Celtic people who inhabited Britain prior to its conquest by the Saxons. In it the author combined Welsh traditions of a bard and prophet called Myrddin with other folklore, legends, and freely interpreted early Latin accounts. His legendary history was purportedly a Latin translation of a "very old book" that related the story of the rise and fall of the Briton people. In deference to his Anglo-Norman readership, Geoffrey changed the name Myrddin to Merlin, and the mystical magician came to life.

MERLIN'S MAGIC TOUCH EASILY RAISES A LINTEL IN ONE OF THE FIRST ILLUSTRATIONS OF STONEHENGE THAT SURVIVES, A FRENCH VERSION OF GEOFFREY OF MONMOUTH'S HISTORY OF ANCIENT BRITAIN.

The chronicler's history began at the very beginning, with the founding of Britain by Brutus, great-grandson of the epic Roman hero Aeneas. By Book Eight of his history, the ancient historian had reached the tales of the war of the Britons against the Saxon invaders. Aurelius Ambrosius, king of Britain, returned from exile in Brittany in about A.D. 460 to recapture his throne.

Ambrosius routed the Saxons in a great battle near Amesbury, then settled the affairs of the kingdom, revived the laws of the land, repaired the churches, and restored peace. He also resolved to avenge the deaths of 460 British lords, all massacred at a monastery near Kaercaradoc—today Salisbury—with an immense memorial to "perpetuate the memory of that piece of ground, which was honoured with the bodies of so many noble patriots." His carpenters and masons declared that they lacked the skills to complete the grandiose monument Aurelius envisioned, and they refused to take on the job.

At that, Aurelius called on Merlin. "If you are desirous," the magician answered, "to honour the burying-place of these men with an ever-lasting monument, send for the Giant's Dance, which is in Killaraus, a mountain in Ireland." He was referring stones that were, so the wizard said, "of a vast magnitude and wonderful quality; and if they can be placed here, as they are there, round this spot of ground, they will stand forever."

Directed by Merlin, the king's brother (who was also Arthur's father), Uther Pendragon, set sail for Ireland with 15,000 men. At Killaraus, the wizard watched as the mere mortals used ropes, cables, and ladders to try to dislodge the huge stones—to no avail. Laughing at their efforts, he easily took down the slabs and had them transported to the ships. The Britons sailed back to England and, amid great ceremony, Merlin used his magic to arrange the stones, just as they had stood in Ireland, around the tomb of the martyred men.

The feat started Merlin on the road to literary immortality and, according to Geoffrey, "gave a manifest proof of the prevalence of art over strength."

# The Mound Builders

## PIONEERS OF ANCIENT AMERICA

CIRCULAR RAMPARTS OF NEWARK EARTHWORKS, ONE OF THE LARGEST GROUPS OF ANCIENT MONUMENTS IN THE UNITED STATES, NOW FORM PART OF THE GOLF COURSE AT MOUNDBUILDERS COUNTRY CLUB IN LICKING COUNTY, OHIO.

# Chapter Two

**WHEN EXPLORERS AND SETTLERS**
pushed beyond the Allegheny Mountains in the 19th century,
they discovered thousands of huge burial mounds scattered
throughout the Ohio River Valley, in present-day Illinois, Indiana,
Missouri, Iowa, and Wisconsin. Who could have constructed such
earthworks—and why? How were they designed, given their
makers' earthbound perspective? Archaeologists have answered many
questions about the ancient mound builders. To do so, they have had
to rely on excavations, for no firsthand written records exist of this first
complex culture to develop in North America. Mound building began
as hunters and gatherers started to turn to agriculture and settle in North
America. Mounds were built over a period of several thousand years by
diverse cultures. They served various purposes and had different
meanings for different peoples. Concentrated along major river systems
in the Midwest, the Southeast, and parts of the East, some mounds were

huge, covering several acres, while others looked like small hills. Some were round, others flat-topped platforms. Still others formed elaborate geometric designs.

The earliest mounds, erected some 4,000 to 5,000 years ago in what is now the southeastern United States, were formed of seashells. They can be found in coastal wetlands, areas rich in natural resources and therefore popular places to settle. The only other shell rings in the Western Hemisphere lie on the Caribbean coast of Colombia. Did ancient Americans travel from South America to present-day South Carolina or Georgia in about 2500 B.C.? Some experts think so, but archaeologists are still looking for evidence to corroborate such a theory.

IN THE CONTINENTAL INTERIOR OF NORTH AMERICA, RIVER VALLEYS ATTRACTED settlers. By 1000 B.C. mound builders were erecting earthworks throughout the Ohio River Valley. When 16th-century Spanish explorer Hernando de Soto traveled through present-day Alabama, the practice of mound building was fading. What brought about the collapse?

By 1800, the mystery of the mound builders was well established. On their way west, Lewis and Clark and their Corps of Discovery stopped to view the earthworks at Grave Creek, West Virginia. No one considered that seminomadic Indians could have built the mounds. In those days, it was rare for anyone to conceive that native North Americans possessed the organization, industry, technology, and intellectual talent necessary to erect such geometric complexities. Soapstone, obsidian, and copper found buried in the mounds fueled the theory that some civilized race, now long gone, had built the earthen structures.

Speculation abounded: The mounds were built by immigrants from Mexico, Phoenician seafarers, wandering Norsemen, the Lost Tribes of Israel, even refugees from the sunken civilization of Atlantis. In the 1840s Ephraim G. Squier and Edwin H. Davis surveyed mounds in the Ohio River Valley. Ultimately they, too, subscribed to the lost race theory.

In 1881 the Bureau of Ethnology within the Smithsonian Institution appointed Cyrus Thomas to study the mounds. Thomas and his assistants devoted four years to surveying, mapping, excavating, and cataloging artifacts from some 2,000 mounds in 24 states. Their careful scientific work demolished the myths of the builders of the mounds. The earthworks, Thomas concluded, were produced by ancient Native Americans of different cultures at different times.

PAINTED MARBLE EFFIGIES ABOUT TWO FEET HIGH, A MALE AND A FEMALE,

ACCOMPANIED A MISSISSIPPIAN BURIAL AT ETOWAH, IN NORTHERN GEORGIA.

ARCHAEOLOGISTS HAVE DISCOVERED ABOUT 350 ELITE BURIALS

IN ONE OF THE CENTRAL MOUNDS AT ETOWAH.

The earliest mounds were constructed during the Archaic Period, between about 4000 and 1000 B.C., when a sedentary lifestyle had become fairly common in eastern North America. Radiocarbon dating of stone projectile points and remains of fish bones, shellfish, and snails have shown that Watson Brake, a site near the Ouachita River in northeastern Louisiana, was begun as early as 3400 B.C. There, 11 mounds, the highest about 25 feet, form a rough oval, most connected by a ridge. The creators of Watson Brake found much of their food in the nearby swamps.

Poverty Point, in the same area, dates from about 3,000 years ago. Its six concentric ridges form a partial oval three-quarters of a mile long. A huge, irregular mound rises 69 feet on the outer edge, and five others lie nearby. Archaeologists estimate that some 600 houses once stood between the ridges, but how many people lived there, how long they stayed, and what they did there are questions that remain unanswered. More than 30 satellite sites in the Mississippi River

PRECEDING PAGES: AN INDIAN MOUND PUNCTUATES MISSISSIPPI'S VICKSBURG

NATIONAL CEMETERY IN THIS HUNDRED-YEAR-OLD GLASS-NEGATIVE PHOTOGRAPH.

THOUSANDS DIED IN THE 1863 CIVIL WAR BATTLE THERE.

Valley have yielded lapidary work, carvings of bird pendants, and other artifacts that indicate trade between mound builders.

FAR FROM THE COASTAL SETTLEMENTS, OTHER MOUND BUILDERS FOUND edible plants and animals and grew corn in fertile river valley soil. Native Americans of the Woodland Period, about 1000 B.C. to A.D. 800, erected mounds in today's Ohio Valley, from Indiana to West Virginia. One great mound near Chillicothe was excavated in 1901 on the Adena Estate, the early 19th-century homestead of Thomas Worthington, governor of Ohio. From that estate came the name for a people: the Adena culture. Adena territory spread in a circle with a 150-mile radius centered in Chillicothe.

Characterized by their special concern for the dead, the Adena began raising monumental conical burial mounds after about 600 B.C. Each mound contained one or more burials. Some held several bodies buried in different ways or in succession. Some bodies were cremated; others, those of the elite, were interred in elaborate crypts constructed of logs. At the two Adena mounds called Robbins Mounds, in northern Kentucky, excavators in 1939 and 1940 discovered that individual graves had been added separately to the margins and top of the mound. These additions widened and heightened the mound so much that eventually its highest point was no longer centered over the cremation remains from the first burial.

Many Adena mounds contain multiple layers. At Cresap, on the Ohio River in West Virginia, burials ranged from simple shallow pits to heavy log-lined tombs. Built between 200 B.C. and A.D. 50, Cresap provides a sequential history of Adena burial practices. Artifacts found in the mound's base—chipped stone tools and bone awls—were all utilitarian. Higher levels of the mound, erected later, contained luxury items such as stone pendants, copper rings, and ornamental silhouettes cut from mica.

Not far from Cresap, near Moundsville, West Virginia, Grave Creek Mound is the largest known Adena burial. One of the first major earthworks discovered by settlers, it is 240 feet in diameter and originally rose 70 feet, about the height of an eight-story building. Erosion had taken its toll by the time Lewis and Clark viewed it: By then, it had shrunk to about 62 feet in height.

The owners of the Grave Creek land began excavating the mound in 1838. One of their finds was an oval white sandstone disc inscribed with 25 strange characters. Some insisted the markings were Phoenician or Celtic, fueling the lost race myth. While this tablet was discovered to be a fraud, about a dozen more such discs have since been dug up at Adena sites. Polished and inscribed with curvilinear designs and bird motifs, the small stone tablets are proof of the achievement of Adena artists. Some experts believe they may have been used as stamps for body or textile paint. Others think they were grinding stones used to sharpen awls or knives used in bloodletting ceremonies.

TALON OF A BIRD OF PREY, AN 11-INCH-LONG ARTIFACT CUT FROM SHEET MICA,
DEMONSTRATES THE WIDESPREAD TRADING NETWORK OF THE HOPEWELL
SOME 2,000 YEARS AGO. ARCHAEOLOGISTS UNEARTHED THE CLAW IN AN OHIO TOMB;
THE MICA PROBABLY ORIGINATED IN PRESENT-DAY NORTH CAROLINA.

One of the mysteries of the Adena is their origin. While they were larger than the peoples who preceded them, some experts have suggested that the Adena developed from earlier native inhabitants. Archaeologists also debate over why Adena culture declined. The Hopewell, another Woodland culture in the same general area as the Adena, emerged after 200 B.C. Some believe the Adena migrated to Mexico, while others theorize that the culture was swallowed up by the Hopewell, which borrowed from it. Others think the Hopewell and Adena developed side by side. No one agrees on the circumstances of the changeover. After the two cultures collided, however, the Adena dwindled and began to vanish around A.D. 100.

THE HOPEWELL ELABORATED UPON THE ADENA ART STYLE, DEATH CULT, AND mound-building practices, developing these cultural features into the height of the Woodland Period. The Hopewell people erected grand ceremonial compounds in various mathematically precise geometrical shapes, with broad plazas and lengthy avenues. Like the Adena, they cremated most of their dead and laid out selected corpses in log crypts. The richness of the Hopewell burials distinguishes their sites from those of the Adena. In 1893 Warren K. Moorehead excavated 15 of more than 30 mounds in a 110-acre earthen enclosure near Chillicothe. The land belonged to a farmer, Cloud Hopewell, whose name came to designate the culture. Moorehead found a rich assortment of copper artifacts—effigies of fish and birds, geometric designs, breastplates, and axes.

The demand by the Hopewell elite for ceremonial objects and burial goods, as well as the resources to make them, fueled an extensive trade network that extended from the Rocky Mountains to the Atlantic and from Canada and the Great Lakes to the Gulf Coast. Obsidian from the Rockies, shells from the Gulf, copper from the Great Lakes, mica from the Appalachian Mountains—all were used in Hopewell grave goods. From their home in southern Ohio, the Hopewell came to dominate much of North America east of the Great Plains. They were the first empire builders of what is now the United States. Rivers were the trade routes that knit their empire together.

A grand system of earthworks, the largest Hopewell ceremonial center, once covered most of the land around present-day Newark, Ohio. Raised ridges of earth formed a perfect circle encompassing 20 acres; parallel embankments linked it to a 50-acre octagon that contained eight burial mounds. A mile to the southeast, more parallel embankments connected a 30-acre circle to a 20-acre square and a gigantic 50-acre oval that held 11 mounds. The two systems were linked by two huge passages enclosed by embankments, and a third roadway led south from the site. Today, only two important features remain at Newark. The great circle, with walls

MYSTERIES OF THE ANCIENT WORLD

8 to 14 feet high, was once used as a public fairground. The octagon is now part of a golf course.

Bradley Lepper of the Ohio Historical Society has studied old maps to reconstruct the complex system and has tentatively plotted a path he calls the Great Hopewell Road. Lepper hypothesizes that a straight avenue linked Newark with another grouping of earthworks nearly 60 miles away in Chillicothe. Some experts insist that the Hopewell lacked the population and organization required to complete such a long-term project. The fundamental mystery of the Hopewell, Lepper argues, is how they achieved feats theoretically beyond their capabilities. He suggests that perhaps those theories are inadequate. More goods arrived in Ohio than ever left it, he points out, suggesting that Newark and other great Hopewell complexes were sacred pilgrimage destinations to which worshipers brought rare and precious offerings.

The second largest Hopewell mound, called Seip, rises 30 feet beside a highway in Ohio. Excavations there revealed a log vault containing the skeletons of four adults and two infants. Buried with them were thousands of pearls, tools, and ornaments of copper, tortoiseshell, and silver. Mound 1 at Seip was the necropolis of at least 132 people. Like many mounds, Seip was virtually destroyed as it was excavated. Archaeologists restored and rebuilt it. Mound City, an early Hopewell site near Chillicothe, also consists of reconstructions. Twenty burials, among them four bodies placed in a grave adorned with sheets of mica, have been restored in the Mica Grave Mound.

Plowing for progress as well as excavations contributed to the destruction of thousands of mounds. In St. Louis, Missouri—early on nicknamed "Mound City"—most burial sites were leveled by the middle of the 19th century. A few communities, like Marietta, Ohio, made a concerted effort to save their Native American heritage. As early as 1788, citizens there set aside the conical Conus Mound as a park.

Fort Hill, a Hopewell site in Ohio, is barely visible, its outlines almost hidden in a dense forest. Unexcavated and unrestored, Fort Hill probably looks as it did in about A.D. 500, at the time when the Hopewell culture was beginning to fade. By that period, many had abandoned their ceremonial sites and moved to villages protected by stockades. Some experts hypothesize that unrest in eastern

North America disrupted the extensive Hopewell trade network and led to the culture's collapse.

Smaller and less elaborate mounds continued to be built in Ohio, but other cultures rose. In Wisconsin and parts of Illinois, Iowa, and Minnesota, Native Americans constructed mounds shaped like men and animals. The mysterious Effigy Mound culture rose and fell rapidly. The Hopewell influence endured, however, and influenced cultures developing in the Southeast. Hopewell-like pottery, figurines, ornaments, and implements have been found in Louisiana, Georgia, and south-central Florida.

One of the mound-builder mysteries that still intrigues archaeologists is the Great Serpent Mound, a quarter-mile-long earthen effigy of a snake in south-central Ohio. Due to its proximity to Adena burials, experts originally thought the Serpent Mound was built by the Adena. Others believed it was Hopewell in origin. Recent radio-carbon dating of two samples of wood charcoal taken from the mound has fueled the controversy. Results indicate that the mound was built about A.D. 1070, about 2,000 years later than previously thought. The mound, insist some experts, was constructed by peoples of the Fort Ancient culture, who lived along the Ohio River and its tributaries in southern Ohio and northern Kentucky from about 900 to 1600. And this mystery grows. Some archaeologists believe the Fort Ancient evolved directly from the Hopewell; others insist that it was part of the Mississippian, a culture that arose at the end of the Woodland Period.

BY A.D. 700 MANY SITES, SUCH AS SWIFT CREEK AND KOLOMOKI IN PRESENT-DAY Georgia, contained mounds with flat tops. This innovation, the platform mound, characterizes the earthworks of the Mississippian Period. Unlike Woodland cultures, which combined a hunting and a farming economy and observed a cult of the dead, the Mississippian culture depended mainly on growing maize. People settled in large villages, often fortified to defend their fields and territory. Their rectangular platform mounds were not used for burials; they served as the bases for temples, chiefs' houses, and other important buildings.

The Mississippian culture—so named because it may have arisen along that river—transformed the North American East during the thousand-year-long Temple Mound Period. The ancestors of the Creek, Cherokee, Natchez, and other Native American groups, Mississippian peoples left behind earthen pyramids 80 to 100 feet high which covered many acres. Platform mounds were often arranged around a rectangular open plaza. To many archaeologists and art historians, the Mississippians' mounds and plazas, the bird and animal motifs in their art, and the particular strains of maize present at their sites all suggest a Mesoamerican influence. Thus far

no artifacts have been unearthed in the Southeast to verify this hypothesis, however. The contact may have been in the form of visits by Mexican traders to the Georgia coast.

By the 11th century A.D. Mississippian sites with dense populations administered by leaders who inherited their positions—societies often called chiefdoms—were scattered across the Southeast and the southern Midwest. By far the largest of these was Cahokia, about eight miles southeast of present-day St. Louis, Missouri, on the Illinois floodplain of the Mississippi River.

Houses, malls, and highways have obliterated much of the original site, but a few hundred mounds may have existed in Cahokia in its heyday, between A.D. 1100 and 1200. Then, Cahokia was a major political and religious center, with a population of perhaps 8,000. It was America's first metropolis north of the Rio Grande. A wooden stockade, two miles long and 12 to 30 feet high, encircled the main community area. In some parts of the site its inhabitants erected five circles, called woodhenges, made of standing cedar posts. Only the postholes remain, but archaeologists have found that posts near the circles' centers marked points where observers could track the sun's progress and mark the solstices and equinoxes.

Cahokia's mounds were arranged around an immense plaza. Of the 80 that survive, Monks Mound—named after Trappists who lived there in the 1800s—dwarfs any other prehistoric construction north of Mexico. Composed of four terraces, it rises a hundred feet and sprawls across more than 14 acres. Mound 72 at Cahokia reveals the elaborate burial style of the elite. The central figure, probably a chief, was interred with an intricate shell blanket, polished stones, arrowheads, and six retainers. A grave nearby entombed 53 females.

One of the finest Mississippian mortuaries for the elite, the Craig Mound, near Spiro in eastern Oklahoma, was lost to science in the 1930s. Looters dug up thousands of artifacts, including copper plates, textiles, decorated pottery, and engraved seashells, then dynamited the mound. The Spiro art that remained—ceremonial axes with handles and blades carved from a single stone, shells engraved with god-animals and birdmen—demonstrated cultural links to two other Mississippian centers, Moundville in Alabama and Etowah in Georgia.

These three sites were the centers of a powerful movement called the Southern Cult, whose world was animated by supernatural beings: horned snakes, antlered fish, winged spiders, a catlike creature with a man's head and a snake's tail. At Moundville, one of the largest Mississippian towns, about 29 flat-topped mounds ringed a huge plaza. A palisade surrounded the site. Residents replaced the wall at least six times over several centuries, suggesting they were defending their territory. Between 1905 and 1906 archaeologists excavated more than 500 burials in Moundville, unearthing discs made of shell and stone and engraved with eagles, winged snakes, and toothy skulls.

Near Cartersville, in northern Georgia, three mounds rise on the northern bank of the Etowah River. The largest, a flat-topped pyramid, stands more than 60 feet high. Here excavations in the late 1800s unearthed copper plaques decorated with winged human figures wearing eagle masks and bizarre headdresses. Burials unearthed in the 1950s revealed more embossed copper plates, as well as a 5-by-15-foot tomb that held disarticulated skeletons of several members of the elite and two seated marble statues.

IN THE 1540S HERNANDO DE SOTO'S EXPEDITION MAY HAVE VISITED ETOWAH. His chronicler describes sighting a grand temple. By 1500, however, the Mississippian culture had faded. Fights and competition for food and land among the mound builders may have led to the culture's demise.

Archaeologists still search for clues to help them further understand and describe these ancient mound-building cultures. Many mysteries remain, but one has been solved beyond doubt. The mound builders were no lost race of heroes. They were Native Americans whose descendants survive today. They were artisans and architects of skill and vision, and they were the founders of the North American continent's first complex culture.

# Mapping the Mounds

By the mid-19th century, burial mounds discovered throughout the eastern woodlands of the United States had been firmly ascribed to a lost race of artisans. The earthworks—and their mysterious origins—attracted hundreds of ardent admirers, among them a young journalist named Ephraim George Squier.

Born in Bethlehem, New York, in 1821, Squier had little formal education, but earned a reputation as a scholar through his own efforts. He worked for several newspapers in the East before moving to Chillicothe, Ohio, at the age of 23. Soon fascinated by the mounds and their artifacts, he would fulfill with dispatch his editorial obligations to the local newspaper, the *Scioto Gazette,* then spend most of his time researching the mounds.

Soon after his arrival in Chillicothe, Squier sought out local physician Edwin Hamilton Davis, known as an expert on the mounds. Born in Hillsboro, Ohio, in 1811, Davis had a lifelong interest in the earthworks and artifacts found in his home state.

Over the next two years, Squier and Davis explored, surveyed, and mapped some two hundred mounds and one hundred earthworks in and around the Ohio River Valley. In 1846 the two men were the first to survey the Serpent Mound in Adams County, Ohio. Near Chillicothe, they investigated Mound City, a 13-acre site that contained more than 23 burial mounds. Squier did most of the writing, prepared the surveys, made drawings of the sites, and tended to arrangements for the publication of the research. Davis undertook the preservation of the several thousand artifacts the team had unearthed and secured financing for their work.

Money and encouragement came from the newly established American Ethnological Society. The pair submitted a manuscript summarizing their research to that group in May 1847. The society lacked the resources to underwrite such a project and turned to the Smithsonian Institution. The research of Squier and Davis appeared in 1848 as the *Ancient Monuments of the Mississippi Valley,* the first publication of the Smithsonian Institution. "No exertion was spared to ensure entire accuracy," promised Squier.

The men described three types of finds: conical burial mounds, earthworks, and pyramidical flat-topped temple mounds. They referred to the geometric earthworks as "sacred enclosures," a concept that anticipated the conclusions of modern archaeologists. The work of Squier and Davis remains valuable; many of the earthworks they so carefully surveyed have long since been flattened. For today and the future, those mounds exist only in Squier's maps and sketches.

**EPHRAIM GEORGE SQUIER DREW CONTOUR MAPS OF PREHISTORIC EARTHWORKS THROUGHOUT THE OHIO RIVER VALLEY IN THE 1840S.**

According to various accounts, Dr. Davis was reserved and somewhat diffident, while Squier was sociable, audacious, and incisive. Perhaps Squier overwhelmed Davis, who was relegated to the secondary role of co-author. The two men certainly disagreed over the crediting of their contributions.

Davis sold the collection of artifacts he believed to be his to an Englishman for a total of ten thousand dollars. Those pieces now reside in the British Museum in London. He continued his studies for some years more, but in relative obscurity. He moved to New York City in his later life and died there in 1888 at the age of 77.

Squier's byline brought him fame and political appointments to South and Central America, but neither longevity nor happiness. He wrote half a dozen more books, all on his travels in those areas. His wife divorced him in 1873, and he was declared insane the following year. In 1888—the same year Edwin H. Davis died—Ephraim G. Squier died, in Brooklyn, New York, just two months shy of his 67th birthday.

UNIFORMED SCHOOLCHILDREN FILE INTO THE TERRA-COTTA WARRIORS AND HORSES MUSEUM, OPENED IN 1994 NEAR XI'AN, CHINA, TO SEE THE LIFE-SIZE ARMY BURIED WITH THE COUNTRY'S FIRST EMPEROR, QIN SHI HUANG DI.

# Standing Soldiers of the Tiger of Qin

## MT. LI

# Chapter Three

SOUTHWEST OF THE CITY OF XI'AN, now the capital of Shaanxi Province in east-central China, hills rise on the south side of the Wei River. One of them, Mount Li, is a tumulus, or artificial hillock, that houses the mausoleum of the first august emperor of China, Qin Shi Huang Di, who ruled China from 221 to 210 B.C. The location of the tomb is important. The area between Lishan Mountain in the south and the Wei River in the north, accorded great feng shui by the Chinese, was valued by emperors of past dynasties. A mile from the tumulus, farmers digging a well in 1974 discovered fragments of terra-cotta statues, a find that has led to one of the largest excavations in Chinese history. A standing army of thousands of life-size soldiers protected the grave of Qin Shi Huang Di. Researchers have uncovered hundreds of attendant tombs and more than 50,000 relics. Millions visit the site each year; in China, only Beijing sees more tourists. Rumors and legends of an underground palace wrap Mount Li in mystery—a mystery that grows as archaeologists unearth more of the site.

From 403 to 221 B.C., as Rome rose in the West, kingdoms warred with one another throughout China. In 246 B.C. a 13-year-old boy, Crown Prince Zheng, inherited the throne of the Qin, or Chi'in, state—one of seven major kingdoms. In 231 B.C. the 28-year-old king began to take control of the scattered states from his headquarters in the village of Xianyang, southwest of Xi'an, where the Yellow River to the east and the Qin Ling Mountains to the south offered natural defenses. Ancient texts say he conquered kingdoms "like a silkworm devouring a mulberry leaf" and forced his rivals to move to his capital. In 221 B.C., having united the warring states for the first time, Zheng proclaimed himself Qin Shi Huang Di, First August Emperor. China probably takes its name from that of his dynasty: Qin, pronounced *cheen*.

An absolute and ruthless monarch, Qin Shi Huang Di became known as the Tiger of Qin. He crushed opposition, dissolved the system of regional landlords, and imposed a central government. The new empire was divided into 36 administrative units, each with a civil governor, a military commander, and an imperial inspector. Qin standardized currency, weights, measures, and writing throughout the country. His subjects toiled to link his realm, building roads, canals, and other public works. The Great Wall was originally attributed to Qin Shi Huang Di, but scholars today believe he restored, consolidated, and connected sections already built.

OBSESSED WITH DEATH, QIN SHI HUANG DI PLANNED A VAST TOMB EAST OF HIS capital. The Chinese believed that each person had two souls. At death the *shen*, or spirit, flew upward to become divine; the *gui*, or ghost, remained underground. Qin Shi Huang Di planned for his gui to rest in luxury. His tomb was also a political statement. The height of a tumulus symbolized the rank of the deceased. As the first emperor, Qin Shi Huang Di demanded a mound that expressed his unique place in history. His tomb was to be the most extravagant in China; the tumulus originally rose nearly 500 feet. Construction may have gone on for as long as 36 years before his death in 210 B.C. It was a massive building project, more a city than a tomb, covering some 20 square miles. More than 700,000 conscripted workers, mostly convicts and prisoners of war, shifted between the various building projects.

Workers dug an enormous terraced pit more than 100 feet deep, then at the bottom built an underground palace, by some estimates 400 by 520 feet in size. After the palace vault, passageways, and side chambers were completed, workers covered all with dirt, topped with the terraced mound that now rises 250 feet above

MAGNIFICENTLY MODELED HORSES BURIED WITH THE SOLDIERS PULLED CHARIOTS AND SERVED THE CAVALRY TROOPS. WHEN DISCOVERED IN 1974, MANY OF THE CLAY STATUES LAY IN FRAGMENTS AND HAD TO BE PAINSTAKINGLY REASSEMBLED.

the surrounding plain of the Wei River. Sima Qian, historian of the Chinese imperial court about a century after the death of Qin Shi Huang Di and first to mention the tomb, described the complex as a microcosm of heaven and earth. It may have been intended as a universe for Qin Shi Huang Di to rule in the afterlife.

"The tomb," wrote Sima Qian, "was filled with models of palaces" along with "precious stones, and rarities." The emperor, dressed in jade and gold, pearls filling his mouth, was laid to rest in a bronze sarcophagus in the central tomb, or palace. Like a site in an Indiana Jones movie, the tomb was honeycombed with false passages and booby-trapped with strung crossbows to discourage intruders. Bronze maps of the world lined the walls. Channels of moving liquid mercury represented the Yellow and Yangtze Rivers. Gems and paintings of stars and planets decorated the tomb's ceiling. Luxury goods and the bodies of sacrificed concubines, slaves, and craftsmen lay in rest, accompanying the emperor to his death.

TODAY THE MOUNT LI TUMULUS RISES OFF-CENTER INSIDE TWO WALLS THAT ONCE surrounded it. A rectangular outer wall of beaten earth with a perimeter of four miles surrounds an inner wall, one and a half miles around. Westerners have known about Qin Shi Huang Di's tomb near the Wei River since the 1920s. French archaeologists published pictures of it in 1924, but it had never been excavated. In March 1974 peasants digging a well unearthed a life-size clay model of a man's head. Then they found more pottery heads, arms, and shattered torsos.

Government archaeologists excavated the trench about a mile east of Qin Shi Huang Di's tomb. They found an immense rectangular pit containing a life-size for-mation of more than 6,000 elite infantrymen, prepared to protect the emperor for eternity. Careful excavation revealed that the pit stretched across more than five acres. Three rows, each with 210 archers and crossbowmen standing shoulder to shoulder, formed the vanguard of the unit, followed by 38 rows of troops, flanking archers on all sides facing outward, and three rows of rear guards. Such a battle formation would make the inner mass of soldiers invulnerable to surprise from any direction, yet the troops could be reconfigured quickly and easily. The armored and helmeted warrior figures carried real bows and arrows, swords, lances, and axes. Their wooden weapons had disintegrated over the ages, but fragments of wood, bronze crossbow triggers, and dozens of arrowheads lay in the trenches. The figures lived up to the legends of the courage and ferocity of Qin Shi Huang Di's soldiers, trained to attack and report-edly paid on delivery of severed enemy heads.

Another pit excavated in 1976 contained a larger variety of soldiers, arranged in a complex battle formation of four separate units of archers, foot soldiers, cavalrymen, and chariots, each drawn by four horses. A third pit resembled a gallery; from clay generals found there, archaeologists presume it was the headquarters for the troops in the first two pits. Deer antlers and animal bones found there suggest it served as a special meeting place where sacrifices and prayers were offered. Some 60 feet west of the tomb, archaeologists unearthed painted chariots of wood and bronze. In 1980 they uncovered a 22-foot-long chamber containing two bronze chariots and horses adorned with silver and gold, the largest and most complicated bronzes yet discovered.

Qin Shi Huang Di's eternal army demonstrates not only his wealth and power but also the skill of his thousands of craftsmen. Each figure was formed of high-fired clay from nearby mountains and baked in kilns close to the pits. And each passed

RE-CREATED TROOPS BAKE PIECE BY PIECE IN A KILN AT A FACTORY ESTABLISHED TO GAIN INSIGHT INTO ANCIENT TECHNIQUES AND TO PRODUCE ITEMS FOR SALE. ABOUT 10 PERCENT OF ALL FIRINGS FAIL DUE TO TEMPERATURE FLUCTUATIONS.

MYSTERIES OF THE ANCIENT WORLD

LARGEST STRUCTURE EVER BUILT, THE GREAT WALL TWINES 4,500

MILES THROUGH THE MOUNTAINS OF NORTHERN AND NORTH-CENTRAL CHINA.

CONSTRUCTION OF THE FIRST SECTION, BUILT TO DETER INVADERS, BEGAN IN ABOUT

690 B.C.; THE TIGER OF QIN ORDERED SECTIONS RESTORED AND CONSOLIDATED.

through four stages—modeling, sculpting, baking, and painting—before taking its place in the army. Every one of the thousands of heads was hollow, formed by pressing damp clay into front and back molds. At least eight standardized head molds were used. Many body parts were mass-produced, but details such as ears, noses, and mustaches were finished individually, making each soldier unique. Sculptors mixed and matched pieces and fashioned a wide variety of armor and clothing, creating a host of warriors of widely ranging ages, homelands, and attitudes. Many of the statues are signed. Archaeologists have deciphered the names of some 85 different master artisans, each of whom had numerous assistants.

Traces of polychrome pigment indicate that each model, including the huge horses and chariots, was individually painted in vivid colors, hues that may have indicated fighting units. Many have been restored. Kneeling crossbow archers found when the second pit was unearthed now have rosy cheeks and sport light green robes and scarlet trousers. The warriors are the earliest examples of life-size, realistic statues found in China. They reside now in the Terra-cotta Warriors and Horses Museum, a spacious, modern complex opened in 1994. A roof over Pit Two allows visitors to watch the excavation and protects the site from the elements. Although most of the statues were found shattered, the army has been pieced together and set up in the positions in which the units were found.

To create the three pits that housed the emperor's army, his workers removed more than 3$^{1}/_{2}$ million cubic feet of earth. Then they tossed soil back into the pits and pounded it into two-foot-thick, rock-hard floors and ten-foot-high perimeter walls, some of which are eight feet thick. The laborers built broad interior walls partitioning Pits 1 and 2 into long corridors. The soldiers of Pit 1 were stationed in 11 parallel bays. Masons then covered the floor with hundreds of thousands of rectangular bricks; those at the center of each aisle were laid higher than those on the sides so that any moisture would drain away from the standing statues.

To protect the terra-cotta army, the builders erected a 7,000-square-yard roof over the pits. They dug foot-deep holes at the base of the perimeter and partitioning walls and erected a heavy cedar or pine post in each hole. They topped the vertical posts with horizontal timbers to form joists. Across the joists carpenters laid 40-foot-long

beams, then covered them with woven bamboo or straw mats and clay layered almost one foot thick. Ramps led up to ground level, and wheel ruts still apparent suggest that large figures were rolled into place. The inclines were later blocked, and the entire vault was buried under almost ten feet of dirt. At some point the roof collapsed, crushing many statues—perhaps in a fire set by rebels just after the emperor's death.

Brutality, forced labor, and exploitation had alienated the people. According to Sima Qian's *Shiji, Records of the Historian,* a Confucian scholar openly criticized the emperor in 213 B.C. In retaliation, Qin burned thousands of books, further damaging his standing. The emperor survived three assassination attempts, but the assaults left him distrustful and reclusive. Intent on obtaining immortality, Qin turned to magicians. At their suggestion, he removed himself from human sight and made it a crime for anyone to reveal his whereabouts.

In 210 B.C., while journeying in search of the elixir of life, Qin suddenly fell ill and died. A few insiders plotted to conceal the emperor's death. According to *Records of the Historian,* rather than notify the legitimate heir of his rightful ascent to the throne, Huhai—one of Qin's younger sons—allied with the emperor's grand counselor, pretended that Qin was still alive, then issued an edict naming Huhai crown prince. When the imperial litter finally returned to Xianyang, reeking in the summer heat, Huhai proclaimed himself second emperor. In honor of his father, he ordered that all Qin's childless concubines and all who had labored on the tomb and knew of its riches be buried with the emperor.

In the late summer or 209 B.C., revolts spread across the empire. Four years after Qin's death, a rebel army set the mausoleum ablaze. An ancient history records that even after 30 days of plundering, the rebels "could not exhaust the contents of the mausoleum. Bandits melted the coffins for bronze as well as setting fire to it. The fire burned for more than 90 days." Archaeologists believe this fire weakened the roof beams over the terra-cotta army. The earthen roof fell, shattering many of the statues and burying them in rubble for 22 centuries.

SINCE 1974, WHEN WELL DIGGERS UNCOVERED THE FIRST HEADS AND SHARDS of Qin Shi Huang Di's army, excavations have continued at Mount Li. The mystery deepens. Why were the soldiers buried here, nearly a mile from the tomb? Why is there no mention of them in Sima Qian's historical record, which details much else about the mausoleum? Perhaps the army was not associated with the tomb, but was instead some kind of war memorial celebrating the unification of China. Was the army standing guard over Qin Shi Huang Di's tomb, or were the clay soldiers meant to protect Xi'an from attacks by the six conquered states to the east? Did rebels really raze Qin Shi Huang Di's opulent tomb, or is it intact?

In the 1980s electronic probes, acoustical soundings, and geophysical prospecting under the mound at Mount Li indicated mercury concentrations up to 280 times normal. Could these be the river models mentioned by Sima Qian? Trenches dug near the tomb revealed that the walls are intact and that the earth covering them has not been moved. Perhaps the early account of the looting of the tomb by rebels is wrong; maybe Qin Shi Huang Di's fabulous grave remains untouched.

Archaeologists have continued to make discoveries. They have located an underground tunnel they consider to be the main entrance into the tumulus. A smaller passage nearby suggests an unsuccessful visit by looters. Almost a hundred pits have

MOST OF THE STATUES SHATTERED WHEN THE ROOF OVER THE PITS COLLAPSED CENTURIES AGO. NOW SKILLED WORKERS PIECE THE EMPEROR'S SOLDIERS TOGETHER. PARTLY ASSEMBLED WARRIORS STAND IN THE BACKGROUND.

been found near the tomb. The three containing the terra-cotta army have been called the eighth wonder of the world. Another pit contained the remains of real horses, buried alive, along with hay to feed them. Some pits contained models of birds and plants, others the remains of human and animal sacrifices.

Years of digging have uncovered an expanding city of the dead outside the Mount Li funeral park. Excavation to the west of the mound in the late 1970s revealed two burial mounds containing the remains of some conscript laborers; more recently archaeologists have unearthed iron collars that shackled them. East of the outer wall surrounding the tumulus, archaeologists have found 17 royal graves. Some of the dead were drawn and quartered, beheaded, or slashed in two—seeming to confirm Sima Qian's account that the second Qin emperor disposed of all his rivals permanently.

Since 1998 Chinese archaeologists have dug small experimental excavations of pits some 650 feet southeast of the mound. They had been puzzled by the lack of any nonmilitary statues among the thousands of figures in the complex, but one of the new sites contained 12 statues of civilians. All heads but one were irreparably damaged, but conservators have been able to restore five models. The figures may represent performers—acrobats, singers, dancers, magicians—and suggest a lighter side of court life with the fierce and single-minded first Qin emperor.

Many of the pieces represent figures in motion, a breakthrough in an art tradition that had not before emphasized the human anatomy. Perhaps the sculptors who created these pieces had been influenced by the art of the ancient Greeks. The same pit contained a 467-pound bronze cauldron decorated with intricate figures of plants and animals. Another held ceremonial armor carved of limestone. Twelve life-size statues found in a third site constitute another breakthrough. Like the entertainers, they reflect the civilian population. With hands crossed at their waists, hats, and long robes, these figures may represent government officials.

TO PRESERVE AND PROTECT FUTURE FINDS, CHINESE OFFICIALS HAVE SLOWED THE PACE of excavation at Qin Shi Huang Di's funeral complex. They have also developed new methods for preserving the artifacts. Paint that had long remained intact curled and peeled off within minutes once a figure was excavated, so conservators researched ways to stabilize the lacquer layer. Now polyethylene glycol, also used by conservators on waterlogged wood, is applied to the statues immediately. Also, more than

**WRIST CLASPED, A RECONSTRUCTED FIGURE STANDS AS A STORYTELLER MIGHT WHEN RECITING. IN ONE OF TWO EXCAVATIONS SINCE 1998, ARCHAEOLOGISTS FOUND 13 NONMILITARY FORMS THAT MIGHT REPRESENT ENTERTAINERS AT THE IMPERIAL COURT.**

two dozen kinds of mold have attacked the models since their discovery. The museum has improved ventilation and uses chemicals to dry the air. A scarcity of funds has slowed digging, along with caution on the part of Chinese archaeologists, who do not want to damage any finds. Experience has demonstrated to them that relics can deteriorate immediately upon exposure to air. Furthermore, mercury can be lethal, and the high levels underneath the tomb could prove an obstacle to excavation.

That mercury, though, adds to the mystery of the tomb. Do the rivers in the grave still flow? Was it looted after the emperor's death? The earth appears undisturbed, so perhaps his tumulus still contains the fabulous treasures historian Sima Qian described. Emperors' tombs—some 30 of them—are spread through the fields around Xi'an. Some experts believe they should be explored first, so that lessons learned in those digs can be applied to the excavation of Xi'an's greatest treasure, the 25-story-high tumulus of the Tiger of Qin. Its legendary marvels have mystified scholars for more than 2,000 years, and for the time being they will continue to do so.

# LEGENDS OF THE TIGER

The man who would become known as the Tiger of Qin first took another name: Shi Huang Di. In 221 B.C., when his armies conquered Qi—the last kingdom of the seven once scattered across China— King Zheng of the Qin announced that he merited a new name. Like most of his actions, the choice was deliberate and calculated.

*Shi* denoted "first," *Huang* meant "august sovereign," and *Di* had come to mean "emperor." In addition to declaring for himself the ultimate in ruling power, the ascending leader chose a name that inspired respect and awe because it referred to a giant of Chinese myth: Huangdi, the Yellow Emperor. According to legend, in China's ancient past, some time in the third millennium B.C., Huangdi had brought order to the Earth and then had risen into the sky as an immortal. By claiming the same name, Qin Shi Huang Di sought that same everlasting life.

Much of our knowledge of Qin Shi Huang Di, China's first emperor, comes from Sima Qian, who lived from 145 to 86 B.C. Considered the father of Chinese history, Sima Qian chronicled his country's past. He wrote *Shiji, Records of the Historian*, about one century after the death of the Tiger of Qin.

In his history, Sima Qian describes the emperor's obsessive search for immortality. The Chinese believed that each body contained two souls, and that to escape, they must be prevented from separating. According to Sima Qian, court advisors told Qin Shi Huang Di that only magical elixirs could extend the life of the body and thus ensure immortality.

Qin Shi Huang Di summoned his magicians and charged them with finding the magic potions. He traveled the empire searching for eight legendary immortals, hoping they might share with him the secrets of everlasting life. These immortals were thought to live in two regions: in the western mountains and on three islands that moved about in the eastern sea. Like the perpetual youths themselves, these eastern islands supposedly dissolved into mist when humans neared. Qin Shi Huang Di sought them relentlessly nevertheless.

"The First Emperor wandered about the shore of the Eastern Sea," wrote Sima

Qian, "and offered sacrifices to the famous mountains and the great rivers and the Eight Spirits and searched for the immortals." About 219 B.C., reported the historian, a native of Qin named Xu Fu and others told the emperor of three spirit mountains in the midst of the sea; they were the islands of the blessed—Penglai, Fangzhang, and Yingzhou.

Xu Fu and his comrades asked to be allowed to fast and purify themselves in preparation, then to sail with a group of young girls and boys in search of the islands. The emperor agreed to this request, equipped Xu Fu and his people with a fleet of ships, and sent the group—3,000 of the empire's finest—in search of the blessed islands.

The expedition never returned. Legend holds that those elite youngsters from

China discovered and colonized the islands of present-day Japan.

Qin Shi Huang Di's magicians never managed to concoct the magical elixir he envisioned, nor did the emperor ever find the immortals and their fabled islands. In one respect he failed in his quest for immortality. In another way, though, he triumphed.

The Tiger of Qin's was one of the shortest reigns through all 2,000 years of dynasty rule in China. Yet few emperors were more influential. One of the most vilified rulers in the history of China, he is also one of the most celebrated. The vast tomb and its silent figures now testify to his legacy. After more than 20 centuries, the Tiger of Qin still looms large in world history.

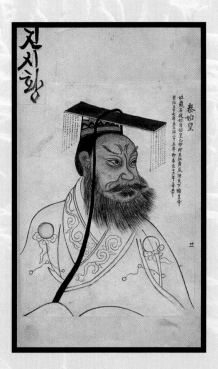

# CHAPTER 4

# *Puzzle of the Pampa*

## PERU'S NASCA LINES

ANCIENT MARKINGS—A TRAPEZOID AND A BIRDLIKE SHAPE—MIX WITH
MODERN SCARS LEFT BY TOURISTS AND TRUCK TIRES WHERE THE
PAN AMERICAN HIGHWAY CROSSES THE PAMPA NEAR NAZCA, PERU.

# Chapter Four

**TWO THOUSAND YEARS AGO** people etched more than a thousand outsize figures in the coastal desert of southwestern Peru. Quadrangles, trapezoids, spirals, narrow lines, and outlines suggesting the shapes of giant creatures stretch through hundreds of square miles of arid plateaus, concentrated between the towns of Nasca and Palpa. The arid surface of the desert—one of the world's driest—made construction of the geoglyphs possible; the static climate has preserved them. The figures were designed over a period of 800 years by the Nasca people, who lived in this area. Since the first trans-Andean pilots spotted the ground drawings from the air in the late 1920s, the Nasca lines have intrigued archaeologists. Why did these ancient Peruvians create designs so immense that they are visible only from the air? How, with only simple technology, did they manage to construct such precise figures? Was there a purpose, a meaning, or a utilitarian plan? Or were these instead decorative embellishments to the gray and barren landscape?

After decades of study, archaeologists have answered some questions, such as how the ancient people built the geoglyphs. The lines seem to have been integral to the culture of the Nasca people, part of a system involving water, planting, and ritual. The Nasca may have used them, too, in their astronomy or their calendar. Some questions have been answered, yet mysteries remain about these intriguing figures.

THREE HUNDRED MILES SOUTH OF THE INCA CAPITAL OF CUSCO, or a 40-minute flight in a small plane, the Nasca lines decorate the pampa—the stony plain-and-plateau region of the country's forbidding and bone-dry desert, which stretches as far as the eye can see. Sandwiched between the Andes to the east and the Pacific Ocean to the west, the region lies in a rain shadow. The Nasca Valley is some 30 miles inland from the Pacific. A low range of hills that stands nearer to the ocean acts as a barrier that stops the eastward movement of the dense and frequent fog that dampens the area closer to the coast. The Nasca region receives at most an inch of rain each year, less than the Gobi or Death Valley.

The main area of the pampa begins about 12 miles north of the town of Nasca. Foothills of the Andes, a series of little hillocks, border the pampa on the east and northeast. The Pan American Highway runs along the base of these hills. The pampa covers approximately 150 square miles, all of it apparently flat and featureless. The ancient ground markings lie in a roughly triangular area between the Ingenio and Nasca Rivers, which cut across the narrow strip of coastal land and carry scant and precious water into the pampa.

Other groups of markings appear on similar level expanses overlooking the Viscas and Palpas Valleys to the north. The abstract look, geometric proportions, and precision of the giant ground drawings add to their allure. Some 800 miles of straight lines and another 300 geometric figures are etched across pampa that is otherwise unmarked. The drawings average 1,300 feet in length and 130 feet in width at the base.

The Nasca created three different types of ground markings, or geoglyphs. The first consist of lines and geometric forms: quadrangles and rectangles, triangles and trapezoids, lines radiating from a common center, zigzags and spirals. Many

WORK HAS PROCEEDED FOR MORE THAN **50** YEARS TO MEASURE
AND MAP NASCA LINES SUCH AS THESE WHORLED FURROWS,
WHICH COMPRISE THE TAIL OF A GIGANTIC ANIMAL FIGURE.

are huge: The largest trapezoid covers 160,000 square yards, and the longest line stretches nine straight miles across the desert. Anthropologists speculate that the spirals depict seashells and represent the ocean, while the zigzags represent lightning and rain, the uncontrollable elements still essential to a people living on this land. In such a desperately dry climate, water was vital to the survival of the Nasca people.

The second type of geoglyph delineated by the Nasca was the life-form, or biomorph. Some 70 figures taken from nature are among the designs etched into the land by the Nasca, and nearly all of these lie in a four-mile square. They populate a single strip of land, the 5 percent of the pampa that lies directly above the southern side of the Ingenio River Valley. In this, the largest and most spectacular concentration of biomorphs, a hummingbird with a wingspan of more

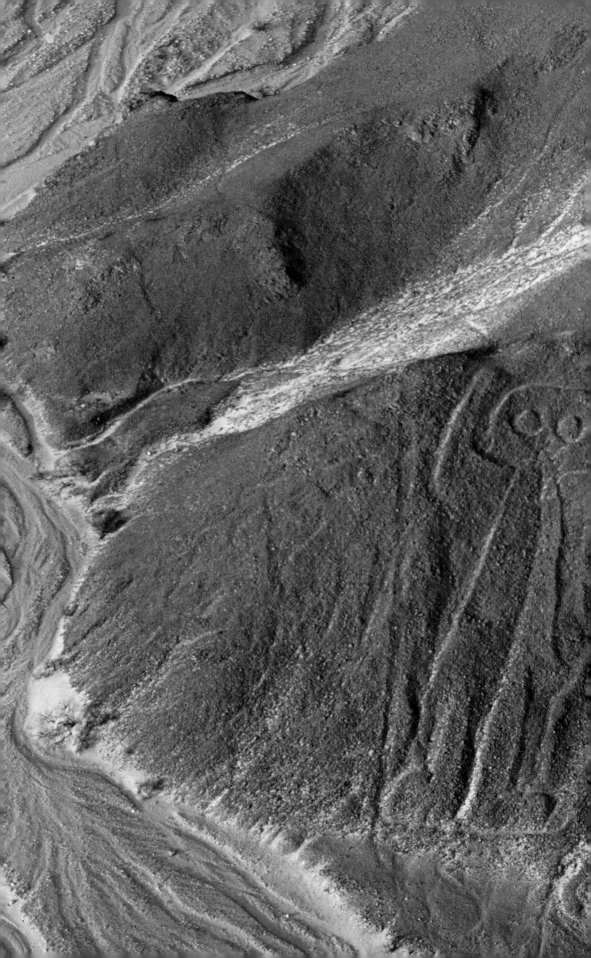

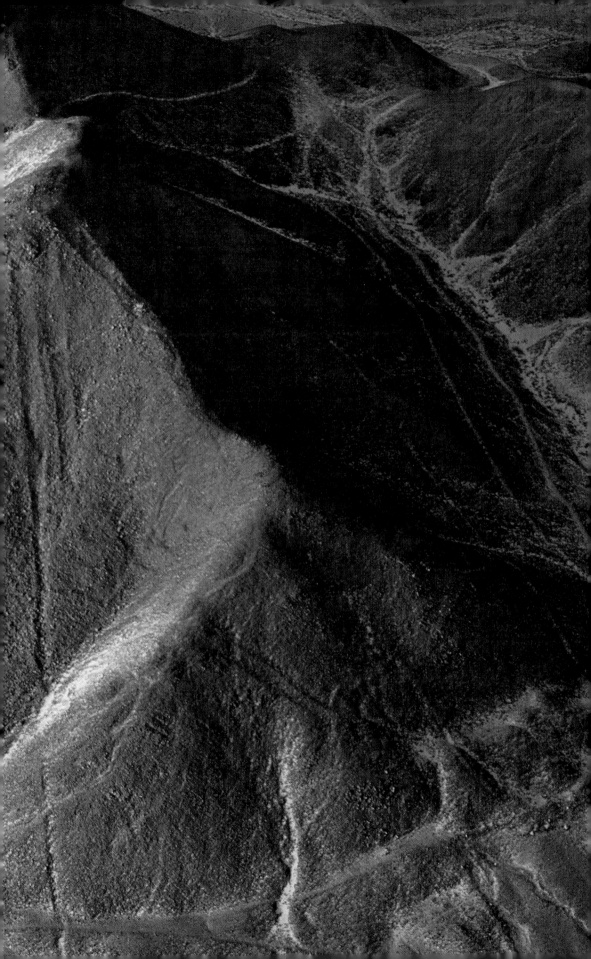

PRECEDING PAGES: NEARLY ONE HUNDRED FEET TALL, THE OWL MAN STRETCHES

UP THE SIDE OF A NASCA HILL, POINTING TO SKY AND EARTH.

ONE EXPERT HAS THEORIZED THAT THIS BIOMORPH REPRESENTS THE MOON.

than 200 feet is one of the smallest of 18 birds designed by the Nasca. A long-necked creature, probably a cormorant, is the largest of the animals. It stretches nearly 2,000 feet from beak to tail. A pelican figure spans 1,000 feet. The vast majority of life forms among the Nasca lines are birds; in Andean mythology they symbolized fertility. Other creatures represented are a 360-foot monkey with a tightly coiled tail, a 150-foot-long spider, several fish, and some strange-looking plants.

Another pictorial geoglyph, the Needle and Loom, stretches 3,000 feet from one end to the other. One of the few human figures among these formations, called the Owl Man, stands close to 100 feet tall, etched into the shallow sloping side of a hill. The figure seems to point to the star Arcturus, prompting some experts to speculate that this hollow-eyed figure represented an intermediary between two worlds.

Many of the biomorphs among the Nasca lines have been damaged. Later tracings of lines have been superimposed on them. One 85-foot-long whalelike figure is cut in half by a line probably made centuries after the cetacean figure. Some specialists argue that the life-forms were executed earlier than the geometric lines: The biomorphs, they hypothesize, were created by the Nasca people and the lines by post-Nasca peoples. In support of this theory, they point out that the configuration of trapezoids and lines seems to exhibit some intellectual organization—probably related to water sources—but the huge drawings of plants and animals as yet defy explanation.

A third type of geoglyph has more recently been defined. These figures, called *campos barridos*—Spanish for swept fields—are flat areas that have been deliberately cleared of surface rock. Some experts believe that the Nasca people created these bare expanses in an attempt to tame the pampa and make it less forbidding.

THE CLIMATE AND GEOLOGY OF THE NASCA AREA MADE THE CREATION of the geoglyphs possible. The rock-strewn surface of the pampa, even 2,000 years ago, was a classic example of desert pavement, a surface of interlocking fragments of boulders, pebbles, or gravel found in arid areas. Desert varnish—a dark coating formed of iron and manganese oxides found on stones in desert regions after long exposure—accumulated on the upper surfaces of the rocks in this region of Peru. The underlying soil, unoxidized, was looser in texture and lighter in color than the surface.

To create their geoglyphs, the Nasca removed the dark, reddish-brown rocks on the desert surface, which had the effect of revealing the lighter-colored, sandy subsurface. They likely moved fist-size pieces of the desert varnish. Farmers in the region today follow the same procedure to create their agricultural fields. Once the pinkish sand was exposed, the Nasca lined it with dark edging, which they made of the oxidized rock, a procedure that made the lines more distinctly visible. The rock borders that line the figures vary from nearly eight inches to almost forty inches in height.

Lines that were left unfinished more than a thousand years ago afford clues to the methods of construction used to create the Nasca geoglyphs. In the middle of partially cleared figures, neat piles of stones still lie, spaced about an arm's length from each other. Researchers believe the Nasca gathered the oxidized stones into piles, moved them to the borders of a figure, then carefully lined up the rocks to create outlines.

To test this hypothesis, in 1984 a group of Earthwatch volunteers re-created the building of a line that ended in a spiral. One group stationed on a hillside sighted the edges of the line and laid out the borders with sticks and ropes. Another—each person spaced an arm's length from the next—gathered all the debris within reach into neat piles. A third crew collected the material from the piles in small containers, moved the stones to the edges of the line, and arranged them as its border.

Working at a leisurely pace, it took only 90 minutes for the group to clear 32 square yards of pampa surface. The Earthwatch exercise proved that the effort required to etch the lines is surprisingly small. A contingent of one hundred people working ten hours a day could have cleared more than 2,000 square yards of dark fragments—the equivalent of a trapezoid some 200 by 10 yards in size—in just two days. This modern crew's accomplishment suggests that a work force of 10,000 laborers could have created all the features on the pampa in less than a decade.

The geoglyphs, experts have established, were not a great feat of engineering, and no advanced technology was necessary to construct them. Material was subtracted from the existing medium, just as it is in the process of etching, and the figures were inscribed into the pampa. Researchers have also determined that the Nasca used another technique—though rarely—to make crude human figures on the steep slopes of hillsides off the pampa. They piled up rocks to create facial features, and then they etched lines away from the surface to represent the rest of the body.

Most of the motifs elaborated on the ground are found in Nasca pottery and textiles. Experts believe that these recurrent images represent the supernatural forces of sky, earth, and water—powers on which the inhabitants of the region depended. The Nasca culture that made its home along the southern coast of Peru flourished from about 200 B.C. to A.D. 600. Its people were not the area's first inhabitants. The area looks desolate today, but ancient peoples once thrived in the river valleys surrounding the pampa. The Nasca lived in large groups of extended families. They survived by fishing the rich coastal waters, hunting in the foothills of the Andes, and farming the land.

Their lines are not the only large-scale archaeological accomplishments that these people left behind. Proof of the level of development of the Nasca is evident in the vast engineering works they built to tame the desert. They constructed a huge network of irrigation channels across the Nasca Valley, many still in working order today. The aqueducts, called *puquios*, are 30 feet deep in some places and a half-mile long. They were carefully lined with cobblestones and emerged in funnel-shaped wells that spiraled into the ground. The canals linked the Nasca River with other waterways descending from the mountains, and they turned the desert fertile.

Little is known of the culture that produced them, though. The Nasca left no written records, nor do any accounts survive that were written by the Spanish conquerors of this region. At the time of the Spanish Conquest, in A.D. 1532, the Indians of the area had recently been absorbed by the Inca Empire. Almost immediately plague, probably brought by the Europeans, decimated the local populations. Wars further reduced their numbers, and within 50 years of Pizarro's appearance on the South American continent, the population of this southern coastal region of Peru was nearly wiped out.

Examples of ceramics and weaving are among the few things that have survived. Nasca culture has long been famous for the beauty of its colorful pottery and textiles. The technological refinement and intricate symbolic decorations of their painted pottery indicate that the Nasca were expert and talented artists. Early Nasca ware lacked much color, but later polychrome pottery was buff or red and painted in many colors. Among the most popular hues were red, black, white, and yellow, with black outlines.

The Nasca maintained an intimate relationship with nature. Some of the decorations on vessels portray everyday activities such as fishing and making

CENTURIES AFTER THEIR CONSTRUCTION, MANY OF THE NASCA LINES THAT TRACE
THE PERUVIAN DESERT HAVE GROWN SO FAINT THAT THEY REQUIRE
CLOSE INSPECTION OR REMAIN VISIBLE ONLY FROM THE AIR.

music. Others, like some of the lines themselves, represent local animals: hummingbirds, killer whales, spiders, and lizards. These features suggest a harmonious existence, but other bits of archaeological evidence gathered over the decades hint that the Nasca were not always peaceful. A common theme of their brightly painted and polished pottery is the depiction of trophy heads taken from their enemies. Severed, mummified human heads, the Nasca thought, were sources of spiritual power.

The life forces of a person resided in the skull, they believed. Human heads were used in rituals, considered fitting gifts for the gods. The Nasca mummified their own dead and buried them in shallow graves. The deceased were placed in the fetal position in wicker baskets and wrapped in cotton shrouds. Wooden dummy heads were sometimes placed on top of the bundles. Alongside the departed ones were buried gifts of food and handiwork. Pottery vessels were generally left as offerings to the dead. Brilliant Nasca funerary ware reflects a level of artistry unsurpassed throughout the Americas.

Pottery is scarce in the valleys, but on the pampa radiocarbon dating of these remains is the most accurate way to determine the age of the geoglyphs. Experts divide Nasca culture into three stages: Early, Middle, and Late. The vast majority of the earth-etched figures were created during the Intermediate Period of the Early Nasca culture, from about 200 B.C. to A.D. 600, after which time the Nasca began to decline. Environmental stresses may have contributed to their downfall; social upheavals or outside invasions may have reduced the population as well. Since no written records exist, such details may never be fully understood.

In the grassy valleys straddling the pampa, archaeologists have found evidence that sheds light on the Nasca. They have unearthed more than 500 habitation sites, surveyed and analyzed them, and determined them to date back to between 500 B.C. and A.D. 1500. Anthropologist Helaine Silverman of the University of Illinois has surveyed and mapped many Nasca sites. In the last decade she has conducted important excavations at Cahuachi, on the south bank of the Nasca River opposite the heaviest concentration of lines. At Cahuachi, which dates from about 100 B.C. to A.D. 400, Silverman has cataloged the remains of more than 40 buildings. The scarcity of artifacts used in everyday living, the remains of ritual paraphernalia retrieved from the site, and the lack of domestic constructions all led Silverman to conclude that Cahuachi was a monumental religious center and pilgrimage shrine of the early Nascas. Depending on the day, Cahuachi could be virtually deserted, or it could be teeming with people and bustling with activity.

Cahuachi's eroding adobe walls of temples, enclosures, and pyramids blend into the desert hills. Tomb robbers have looted most of the hundreds of burials that have been unearthed during recent study, but skulls, teeth, hair, and skin-covered bones of inhabitants do remain. Silverman's discoveries, along with pottery shards and radiocarbon-dated organic material removed from within and below the desert varnish, seem to confirm that the lines were the creation of the Nasca people who lived—and probably worshiped—here.

THE MOST INTRIGUING QUESTION REMAINS, HOWEVER: WHY WERE THESE massive and mysterious figures constructed? Theories are almost as numerous as the puzzling patterns on the pampa. To visualize and create the giant drawings, our modern sensibility tells us, the artists must have soared over the pampa in primitive gliders or hot-air balloons. In fact, some people have explained the mysterious lines as signals to ancient terrestrials. In his 1968 bestseller, *Chariots of the Gods,* Swiss author and explorer Erich von Däniken promoted the idea that the gigantic trapezoidal figures of the Peruvian pampa were runways on which precursors of modern alien abductors once landed their spaceships.

Others have maintained that ancient athletes built the zigzags as venues for competitive footraces. Perhaps the geoglyphs were fashioned as effigies of ancient animal gods. Maybe they comprised a huge astronomy book, noting and plotting patterns of constellations important to the Nasca. Some observers have fantasized that the drawings were a memorial to a long-forgotten atomic war, a calculator of tides, or a global map of ancient trade routes.

Less imaginative—yet perhaps more sensible—theories suggested that the patterns pointed to specific stars, such as Arcturus, to which the big-eyed Owl Man seems to gesture. If so, were the figures a stellar template or an analog star map in which each effigy represented a real star pattern at a certain time of the year? Or is the answer more pedestrian: Were the markings simply roads? Some of the most recent studies have suggested that the lines were ritual pathways or indices of water in the desert. The attempt to answer the "why" of the Nasca lines continues. Researchers have worked for decades, but a definitive answer still eludes them.

Worldwide interest in the Nasca lines dates back to the late 1920s. When regular commercial air flights began between the cities of Lima and Arequipa, to the south, passengers as well as pilots began reporting their sightings of large cleared areas in the Nasca region. The first investigation of the geoglyphs is attributed to Peruvian archaeologist Toribio Mejía Xesspe, who explored and excavated in various valleys of the Nasca River in 1927. According to local lore, as Xesspe stood on a barren hill overlooking the pampa, he spied a maze of lines

traced on the desert plain. Soon thereafter, other lines were noted and identified throughout the entire area.

In 1940 Xesspe published his findings and offered two theories to explain the mysterious lines. Xesspe hypothesized that the lines were pre-Columbian religious or ceremonial roads. He also proposed that they were associated with an ancient irrigation system that he had also discovered in the region. As researchers have continued to assess the Nasca markings throughout the 20th and into the 21st centuries, Xesspe's theories have proven increasingly valid.

IN 1939 AMERICAN HISTORIAN AND GEOGRAPHER PAUL KOSOK TRAVELED to Peru to study ancient irrigation systems in the northern part of the country. Intrigued by reports of pre-Hispanic canals at Nasca, Kosok, a professor at Long Island University, and his wife, Rose, traveled south to see them. Kosok realized immediately that the markings were not canals, but he still recorded many of them: straight lines, spokelike arrays of lines, outlines of huge animal figures, and lines forming enormous trapezoids that enclosed a cleared space.

On June 21, 1941, Paul and Rose Kosok were enjoying a picnic on the pampa near the Palpa River Valley. In the late afternoon of that last day of the Southern Hemisphere's winter, they watched the sun set almost directly over the end of one long line. Inspired by the celestial occurrence, the Kosoks determined that the lines had an astronomical purpose. "We realized at once that perhaps we had found the key to the riddle," wrote Paul Kosok of that evening. "With what seemed to us 'the largest astronomy book in the world' spread out in front of us, the question immediately arose: How could we learn to read it?"

Kosok pioneered the use of aerial photography to trace the lines and gather an overall impression of them. With the assistance of the Peruvian Air Force, he directed the first scientific exploration of the markings. Then Kosok elaborated on his "astronomy book" theory, arguing that Nasca astronomers had noted the same phenomenon at different spots on the pampa and that other lines might point to the Pleiades, the bright cluster of stars in the constellation Taurus.

Maria Reiche, a German mathematician, took up Kosok's astronomical hypothesis and continued his work. For more than 50 years Reiche trekked and

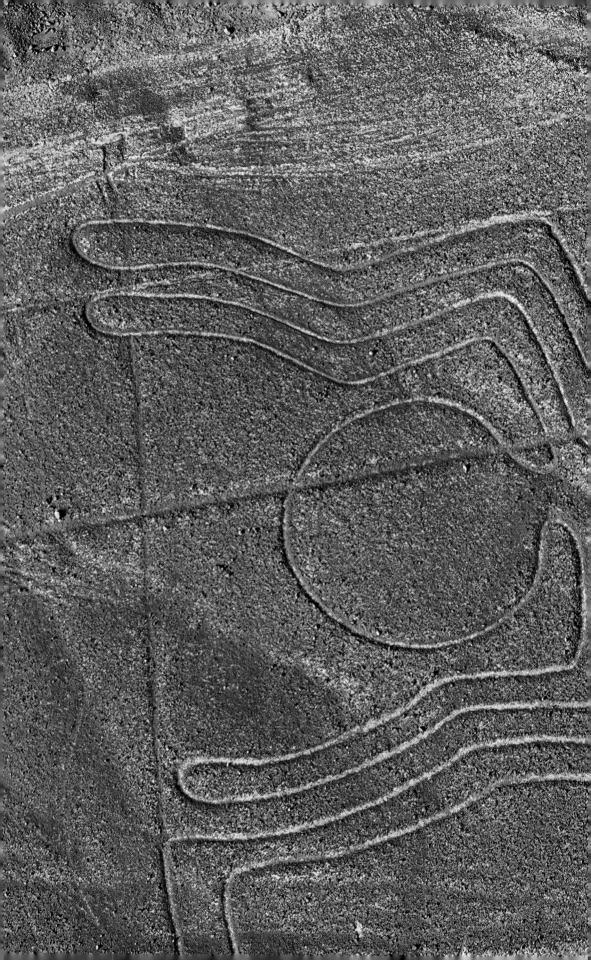

mapped, cleared and guarded the geoglyphs as she searched for evidence of stellar and solar alignments. At her request, a lookout tower was erected along the Pan American Highway so that curious tourists could view the geoglyphs without trampling the soil.

Until her death in 1998, Reiche clung steadfastly to the idea—now much criticized by scholars—that the Nasca figures marked the positions of stars, the sun's position at the solstices, and certain other significant positions of the sun and the moon. The lines and their directions, she insisted, served as an astronomical calendar that helped the Nasca people determine when to sow and when to reap. As to the animal and plant figures—which are relatively few in comparison to the straight-line figures—she speculated that each of them may have had "significance as a totem and/or stellar image."

In 1967 the British astronomer Gerald S. Hawkins turned his sights on the Nasca lines. Hawkins had just completed his study of Stonehenge, in which he used a mainframe computer to plot solar and lunar alignments at the site and had concluded that it was an ancient observatory. Now Hawkins used a computer to recreate the changing map of the sky in the Nasca region of Peru over the previous 7,000 years. By calculating that only 39 lines coincided with the movements of the sun and the moon and that 80 percent of the geoglyphs were unrelated to the movements of the 45 main heavenly bodies in the sky above them, Hawkins cast serious doubts on any astronomical interpretations.

ANTHONY F. AVENI, PROFESSOR OF ASTRONOMY AND ANTHROPOLOGY AT Colgate University, also consulted a computer to search for solar alignments among the Nasca lines and concluded that the lines had nothing to do with astronomy. Aveni, who helped found and develop the field of archaeo-astronomy, began his research into the Nasca lines in 1977. He had already studied the *ceque* system, a radial scheme by which the Inca people of Peru partitioned their capital into kinship and irrigation zones. Wrapping up a season of fieldwork in Cusco, Aveni and his associate, R. Tom Zuidema, decided to drive 300 miles south over the Andes to visit Nasca's famous lines for the first time. Later, as the two men flew over the area in a dusty Cessna, they noticed

COMMON MOTIF OF NASCA POTTERY AND TEXTILES, ZOOMORPHIC CREATURES WITH FELINE AND HUMAN ATTRIBUTES REMAINED A POPULAR THEME IN COASTAL PERU FOR CENTURIES. THIS WEAVING DATES FROM BETWEEN A.D. 1350 AND 1500, A TIME WHEN TEXTILES CIRCULATED LONG DISTANCES THROUGH TRADE AND PILGRIMAGE.

spokelike patterns on the ground below them. Back in the States, Aveni began to ponder the markings that they had seen.

With Zuidema and another associate, Gary Urton, Anthony Aveni studied aerial photographs of the lines and maps of the pampa produced by Maria Reiche. The men were immediately struck by the resemblances between the spokelike patterns of straight lines that the Nasca had etched into the desert by around A.D. 500 and the radial plan of Cusco's Inca ceque lines created about a thousand years later.

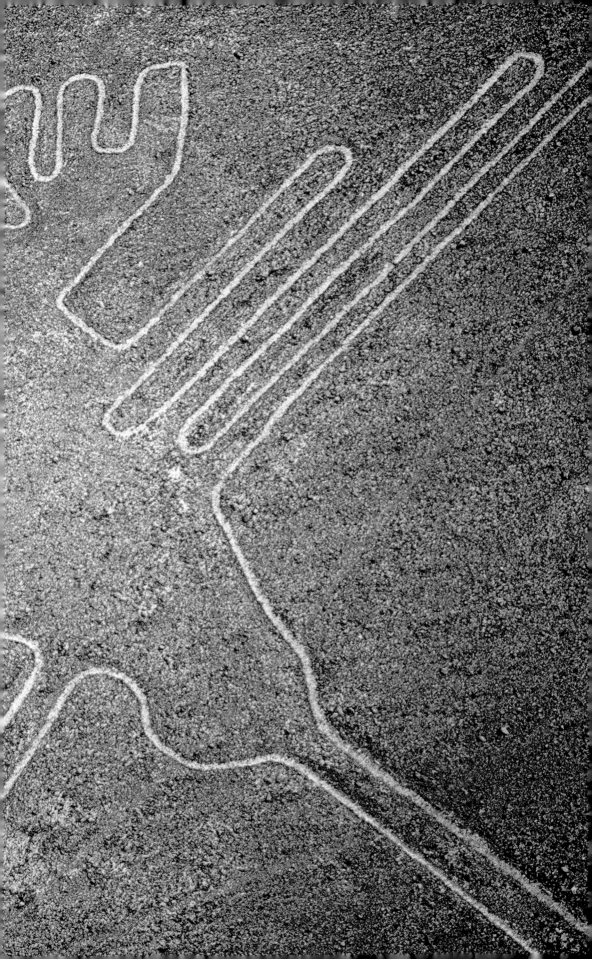

PRECEDING PAGES: A 350-FOOT-LONG HUMMMINGBIRD ETCHED ON THE PAMPA

SEEMS TO SUCK NECTAR FROM A DRY RIVERBED. MANY DRAWINGS

AMONG THE NASCA LINES ECHO DESIGNS ON THE CULTURE'S COLORFUL POTTERY.

The Inca, according to Spanish chroniclers, split their capital into four sectors, called *suyus,* the divisions between them marked by roadways.

Cusco's ceque system was basically a map imposed on the city, shaped like a huge spoked wheel. Its many aspects were interwoven parts of a complex plan, and water was critical to the entire system. Forty-one imaginary lines emanated from the Temple of the Sun and organized the city politically, socially, and geographically. Along those lines were arranged *huacas,* or places sacred to the people. Cusco's ceque system was such a highly organized plan, the three archaeologists hypothesized that it must have had a less sophisticated precursor. They wondered if the radial Nasca lines prefigured Cusco's system.

BACK AT COLGATE, AVENI AND URTON STUDIED THE PATTERN OF THE PAMPA across the ten-mile stretch between the Ingenio and Nasca Rivers. They concentrated their attention on the centers where lines met and the points where lines intersected. Armed with maps and photographs, they returned to Nasca. Despite temperatures of 100°F at midday, amid blowing sand, their eyes blurred from salty perspiration, the two men traced on foot the rough patterns of lines that spread along the Nasca River. Working with a team of volunteers, Aveni and Urton mapped and measured the lengths, widths, and precise orientations of 762 lines that emanated from 62 centers. Lines and line centers, they found, were by far the most dominant features etched into the pampa. And the line centers resembled one another. Each was a natural hill or mound, and each was usually topped with a cairn.

The geographic position of the radial centers was significant, they found. Almost every center either lies on the last hills of the series that protrude from the foothills of the Andes onto the pampa or it rises from high dunes that flank the Ingenio, the Nasca, and their tributaries. The centers lie at strategic points where water flows into the river valleys that abut the pampa.

Standing at each mounded center, an observer could see a long distance, 360 degrees around. A dozen or more lines radiated outward in all directions to the horizon. About a quarter of them were connected to other centers. Many of the lines opened into huge trapezoidal geoglyphs; many of those trapezoids' axes had been oriented along the watercourses. Aveni and Urton discovered that two-thirds of the narrow ends of the trapezoids pointed upstream, and that the wider bases of the figures often aligned with the banks of rivers and their tributaries. For anyone walking along the line, the upstream direction of the water flow invariably lay to the right. Even in the dry season, an observer could determine the direction from which water would flow onto the pampa. Such findings convinced Aveni and Urton that the construction of the lines was intimately connected in some way with water.

Like Gerald Hawkins, the men discovered no obvious connections between the lines etched into the desert and astronomical bodies that shone in the sky above

BUFF AND BROWN, TWO POPULAR COLORS IN NASCA POTTERY, DECORATE A
STIRRUP-SPOUT JAR THAT MAY DEPICT A MONKEY. NASCA CRAFTSMEN
DID NOT USE SHADING AND OUTLINED EACH COLOR IN BLACK.

them. They did, however, find that some lines intersect the part of the horizon where the sun rises in late October and early November—the season in which water begins to run in the pampa rivers. This discovery prompted yet another question: Could the Nasca have used solar observations based on their lines to anticipate the flow of water on the pampa?

While these hypotheses suggest practical uses for the lines, Aveni and Urton became convinced that the lines played an important part in the spiritual life of the Nasca. The lines connected sacred sites and marked ritual pathways. The archaeologists found remains of footprints, which have proven impossible to date, on nearly every line. Perhaps, as in Inca Cusco, different groups of people were allowed to use the water at different times of the month. Perhaps each line was assigned to a specific kinship group, whose members would walk that line at a given time of the year to tend to the group's need for water. Just like the sacred huacas arranged along Inca ceques, the Nasca line centers may have been important ceremonial sites. Aveni's research has convinced many experts that the lines were meant to be walked—that they served ceremonial purposes and plotted the routes of pilgrimages as well as everyday travel routes in the lives of the Nasca people.

LIKE AVENI, ARCHAEOLOGIST JOHAN REINHARD, NOW A NATIONAL GEOGRAPHIC Society Explorer-in-Residence, concludes that the Nasca lines were sacred pathways to sites where water sources were worshiped. The association of mountains, water, and fertility is a persistent belief throughout the Andes. The mountains near Nasca are not the high and snowy peaks of the central range, yet Reinhard saw associations between the myths and beliefs of the two regions. He studied colonial accounts of traditional worship, current beliefs rooted in the distant past, and local myths. All suggest that the basic Nasca beliefs appear to have been similar to those of other Andean peoples.

The first to theorize the lines' relation to sacred rituals involving water, Reinhard argues that the geoglyphs were part of a religious complex designed primarily to ensure crop fertility. The Nasca people believed that mountain gods protected humans and controlled the weather, thus affecting the fertility of the land. The Nasca considered the ocean itself a source of fertility for land and for animals. They considered the mountains as sacred.

Spanish chroniclers in the late 16th and early 17th centuries wrote that the ancient Nasca worshiped on a mountain of sand. The only white sand mountain near Nasca is Cerro Blanco, which—Reinhard holds—had mythic connections to subterranean water.

The Nasca associated higher mountains, especially one called Illakata, with the lord of meteorological phenomena. According to one myth, Cerro Blanco was the wife of Illakata. She came down from the highlands to visit the coast, where she tarried too long and tried her husband's patience. The sun burned Illakata's wife, turning her into stone and sand; she remains there forever as Cerro Blanco, literally the white hill.

Reinhard first suggested a link between ancient geoglyphs found in northern Chile with the worship of mountain-water gods. There, at a site called Cerro Unitas, two-mile-long straight lines stretch across the valleys and up to hills on which fertility offerings were made. Anthropomorphic figures at Cerro Unitas are closely associated with extensive irrigation systems built to distribute the water that emerges from the nearby Andes Mountains, sacred to the people living there.

In the Nasca region as well, Reinhard points to the link between a pale, barren hill near the desert geoglyphs and a major snow-covered peak in the Andean highlands. Such mountains, he attests, are still believed to be the principal deities controlling weather and fertility.

In Puquio, a town 50 miles from Nasca that has had close contacts with it for several centuries, ritual specialists climb a nearby mountain every August to make offerings in hopes of receiving the gift of water. The people of Puquio believe the most important local deities reside in the mountains, and that they are responsible for the fertility of the fields and the livestock. The village's very name comes from the local word for aqueduct.

Reinhard also analyzed the Nasca lines, paying attention to the themes of mountain gods, water, and fertility still prevalent throughout the Andes. Bird figures—like the intricate Nasca hummingbird and the condor—are believed to be symbols of faithfulness to the mountain gods. Monkeys represent the hope for water, while spiders and plants are associated with rain.

Reinhard surveyed sites in three countries up and down the Andes Mountain range—Peru, Bolivia, and Chile. He accumulated evidence that the Nasca figures, although by far the most elaborate and complex of all examples, belong to a more widespread Andean practice of line- and figure-drawing designed to propitiate nature gods and ensure productive harvests. Even today, Bolivian villagers walk a straight line of stones to a hilltop shrine while dancing and praying for rain.

AIDED BY A GRANT FROM THE NATIONAL GEOGRAPHIC SOCIETY'S COMMITTEE
for Research and Exploration, Helaine Silverman conducted research along the
south coast of Peru in 1988 and 1989, surveying the Ingenio and middle Grande
River Valleys. In addition to excavations at the ceremonial site of Cahuachi,
Silverman and her team identified 69 new ground markings on the valley hillsides.
Valley and pampa geoglyphs were dated based on the earliest pottery shards found
at each figure. The data indicated that the vast majority of the ground markings
were created by Nasca peoples during the Early Intermediate Period (circa 200 B.C.
to A.D. 600). Previously, other scholars had argued that the figures were etched
significantly later. Some experts still believe that the biomorphic shapes
predate the lineal geoglyphs by several centuries and may be clan symbols.

Silverman refers to contemporary Andean concepts to explain the glyphs
created by the ancient Nasca people. The word *pampa* in Quechua, the Inca
language, refers to unbounded natural space; *kancha* delineates the opposite: a
bounded or defined unit of space. The geoglyphs of the Nasca, Silverman believes,
converted open, natural space into bounded cultural space, turning the pampa
and the valley hillsides into human and controllable space. They brought
the desert and nearby valley hillsides under human control and transformed the
pampa from an untamed no-man's land, an obstacle to be crossed, into a
pilgrimage route integral to the Nasca religion.

According to this theory, each glyph was created and maintained by a distinct
group or political unit. Those people worshiped there; the markings became sacred
and came to represent that particular group. After a Nasca social group had used a
glyph repeatedly, they might actually abandon that design and etch a new one, which
explains the imposition of newer lines over older ones in many of the figures.

Among the settlements identified by Silverman's survey project was a discovery
called Field Site 165. Almost directly north of the ceremonial center of Cahuachi,
and connected to it by a lineal geoglyph, Site 165 is composed of hundreds of
habitation terraces and several large enclosures. It contains the remains of walled
buildings and a few artificial mounds.

The site, greatly damaged over the centuries due to agricultural expansion, once
stretched some two miles along the south side of the middle Ingenio River Valley.
Site 165 continued to be occupied after Cahuachi declined, in about A.D. 400.

It may have been a city, housing an urban population not found at the ceremonial site. Or, the settlement may have absorbed the local population of the river valley. Further excavation may answer some of the questions its discovery has provoked.

Silverman theorizes that Cahuachi and Site 165 were the dual capitals of the Nasca people. Further, she proposes that the geoglyph-etched pampa was the communications and pilgrimage route between the two settlements and from those settlements to other sites in the valleys on the northern side of the pampa.

"Pilgrims danced, tranced, and masked on and across many of the straight, zigzag, and figural markings in addition to marking the pilgrimage route with stone cairns and new lines," says Silverman. The lines, she concludes, were essential to Nasca society and were an integral part of the culture. They served many functions: They were ceremonial roads, pilgrimage routes, a ceque system that predated that of the Inca, and water and fertility cult markers.

INDEPENDENT SCHOLAR DAVID JOHNSON HAS WORKED ON THE PAMPA for more than a decade. He is especially interested in the ancient aqueducts, or puquios, that ring the area. A vast system of channels carefully lined with cobblestone, these man-made waterways were constructed at about the same time as the most prominent straight lines on the pampa. A trickle of water still flows through the ancient channels: As moisture from the Andes sinks through cracks in the bedrock, it is carried in deep fractures down into the valleys.

Working with associates from the University of Massachusetts, Johnson has developed a theory that the lines, and especially the trapezoidal figures, map underground water sources, not surface ones, as Anthony Aveni has proposed. The desert-dwelling Nasca, insists Johnson, had ways to determine where aquifers existed. They intentionally settled near the underground acquifers and built the puquios to capture the water. To record their discoveries, they etched drawings on the pampa, marking the location, extent, and direction of underground water flow. Researchers continue to attempt to prove Johnson's theory. Given the intricacy of the lines, though, many experts consider his suggestion too simple to explain the many markings on the ground. They also doubt that a preliterate people such as the Nasca would have had the knowledge to find and map aquifers.

Some scholars still search for an astrological solution to the significance of the lines. Phyllis Pitluga, senior astronomer at the Adler Planetarium in Chicago, has broken down the biomorphs into types, such as birds and plants, and has

**TRAPEZOIDS AND LINES—ANCIENT MARKINGS LARGE AND SMALL—ETCH THE DUSTY PAMPA OUTSIDE NASCA. BEYOND THEM THE GREEN OF IRRIGATED FIELDS SWEEPS TO THE FOOTHILLS OF THE ANDES.**

POLYCHROME, SLIP-PAINTED BEAKER REFLECTS THE SKILL OF NASCA ARTISTS, WHOSE WORK GREW MORE COMPLEX IN COLOR AND DESIGN OVER TIME. NASCA POTS AND BEAKERS WERE BUILT OF COILED CLAY AND PAINTED WITH UP TO EIGHT BRIGHT COLORS MADE FROM MINERALS.

studied the straight lines associated with each group. Pitluga found that each set of lines pointed to dark spots in the Milky Way galaxy—spots that modern Andean people identify as pictorially similar to a biomorph associated with it. For example, Milky Way silhouettes that people say are birds line up with bird biomorphs.

Further, the alignments occur at significant periods in the year. The Nasca people would have used the lines, says Pitluga, "twice a year, to show the coming of water and to celebrate harvest time." Although her theory, when applied to the bird type of biomorph, seems to accommodate the elements of water, harvest, irrigation, the gods, the calendar, and astronomy, in fact some lines do not line up in the same way. A whale geomorph points to a silhouette that Andeans see as a serpent. Pitluga formulated her theory after having studied only 28 of 70 biomorphs.

Anthony Aveni remains firm in his belief that the lines were related to water. "If astronomy is present," he insists, "my tentative conclusion is that it's in a slight excess of lines pointing to the place on the horizon where the sun rises and sets around November 1." That date marks the approximate beginning of the rainy season, a time of year when the ancient Nasca people might have made offerings to their rain gods.

All students of the Nasca culture agree: These mysterious people developed imaginative and powerful methods by which they were able to order their lives, make the best use of the natural resources around them, and assure their place within the cosmos. Experts have solved many of the puzzles of the lines. Most now agree that they had multiple functions—practical and religious, social and political, cultural and geographical.

These outlines lay undisturbed for perhaps 2,000 years. In the intervening centuries, grave robbers and gold diggers, jeeps and dune buggies, and tourists on foot have all left their marks on the legacy of the Nasca culture. Built in the 1940s and 1950s, the Pan American Highway now threads the area. It contributed more scars: It actually bisects a lizard biomorph.

Threats to the lines continue to grow. Ankle-deep trash obliterates some of them. Illegal gold mines proliferate near others. The Peruvian government lacks the funds to protect the site adequately. In July 2003, cargo trucks were caught cutting across the lines to avoid paying tolls on the highway. In 2004 one conservationist identified yet another danger to the markings: Desertification is allowing water to wash away some of the lines. Despite the threats, however, hundreds of the mysterious markings endure, as do the compelling questions that they evoke.

# THE LADY OF THE LINES

The locals of Peru's Nasca region originally referred to Maria Reiche as "the crazy foreign woman." Decades of solitary research and care for the soil lines earned her a new nickname: "the lady of the pampas."

Reiche, born May 15, 1903, in Dresden, Germany, was the daughter of a pioneer feminist. Her father died when Reiche was 13; his widow raised Maria, her ten-year-old sister, and a younger brother.

In 1932, at age 29, Reiche took a job as governess in the home of the German consul in Peru. She left Germany as Hitler's Third Reich gained strength. She started cataloging ancient mummies for archaeologist Julio Tello in Lima. Toribio Mejía Xesspe, who had explored and excavated in the Nasca area, took Reiche on a field trip to the pampa in 1939. In 1941 she met American archaeologist Paul Kosok, who hired her to translate his work into Spanish.

Kosok was convinced that the lines of Nasca had an astronomical purpose. His hypothesis captivated Maria Reiche—it combined her intellectual interests in mathematics, antiquities, and astronomy. As a German, she was confined to the city of Lima for the duration of the war. She had to wait until 1946 to begin her own investigation of the lines. In the fall, funded by Kosok, Reiche departed for Nasca. Only the major features of the lines were visible. She cleared many of them with a broom and rake.

Reiche began her work as an outcast. She lived first in an adobe hovel off the Pan American Highway and hitchhiked 12 miles to her archaeological site. Then she moved to a room in a primitive San Pablo ranch—and walked an hour to the figures she was studying on the edge of the Ingenio River Valley. She hiked miles of the pampa daily, noting each line and its position. Mice chewed holes in her personally plotted charts and her pages of calculations. To preserve them, she hung them from clothes pins suspended from the ceiling of her room, a practice she continued until her death.

Save short trips to the outside world, Reiche spent the rest of her life in the solitary pursuit of studying, mapping, and preserving the mysterious markings on the pampa. She was an eccentric. For years she ate the same meal—bananas, jam, and milk—three times a day and seven days a week. She noted some of her precious

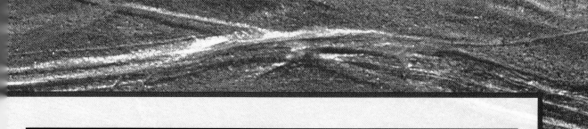

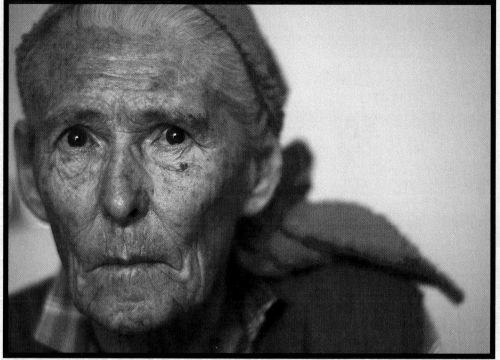

**WEATHERED AND WORN FROM A HALF CENTURY OF WORK IN THE PERUVIAN DESERT, MARIA REICHE PATIENTLY STUDIED AND FIERCELY GUARDED THE NASCA LINES UNTIL HER DEATH AT 95.**

calculations for posterity on toilet paper. She was a recluse, deliberately avoiding social interactions and hiding most of her data in boxes under her bed.

But Reiche was also charismatic. She won the respect and support of locals to her cause and earned considerable help from them. Parkinson's disease slowed her efforts in the last years of her life; glaucoma rendered her nearly blind. She cantankerously blocked others from "her" site. But she was devoted, and her hard work was admired even by those she thwarted. Her first adobe house became a museum. She was given Peru's Order of Merit in 1977, then in 1993 its highest award, the Order of the Sun. When she died of cancer in 1998, she was mourned by archaeologists around the globe as well as by the locals who had once called her crazy. Peruvian schools close in honor of her birthday, and a postage stamp has been issued to memorialize her.

# Sentinels of Rapa Nui

## EASTER ISLAND

BELOW MOAI AT AHU NAU NAU, HORSEBACK RIDERS POUND ACROSS THE BEACH
AT ANAKENA ON THE NORTHERN COAST OF EASTER ISLAND. THE STATUES WEAR
DISTINCTIVE HEADDRESSES, CALLED PUKAOS, MADE OF RED VOLCANIC ROCK.

# Chapter Five

EASTER ISLAND, RAPA NUI IN THE
language of its people, is the most isolated inhabited spot on
the Earth. The easternmost of the 287 islands that comprise
Polynesia, it lies more than 2,000 miles off the South American
coast west of Chile and 1,400 miles east of Pitcairn Island, its
nearest inhabited neighbor. More than a thousand years ago, the
people of Easter Island lived alone in the vast emptiness of the
64-million-square-mile Pacific Ocean. On a volcanic triangle of land
about the size of Washington, D.C., they raised hundreds of carved
many-ton monoliths—called *moai*—that have intrigued archaeologists
since their discovery some 300 years ago. Admiral Jacob Roggeveen,
sailing for the Dutch West India Company, sighted Rapa Nui on Easter of 1722.
From that Sunday on, Easter Island's gray stone sentinels have raised many
questions. Who settled this island in the middle of nowhere? Where did the
settlers come from, and how did they negotiate and navigate the uncharted
and open expanses of the Pacific? Were the people of Rapa Nui isolated on

PAGE 130: HER POLYNESIAN HERITAGE EVIDENT, A MAIDEN DANCES AT

AHU TONGARIKI, ON THE SOUTH COAST OF EASTER ISLAND. TOURISM ABOUNDS;

FOUR FLIGHTS A WEEK LAND AT MATAVERI AIRPORT IN PEAK SEASON.

their small volcanic bit of land, or did they maintain contacts with their homeland? Who carved the giant statues? And why? What do the brooding stone sentinels mean? How did a people lacking technology move the monoliths? When Europeans first viewed the gigantic statues, they were lying head-down in the earth of the island. Why, once carefully raised, had they been toppled from their altars? What caused the end of the culture that had worked so hard to erect the stone wonders?

Few of these mysteries could be solved. The Rapa Nui culture lacked a written history, and firsthand information was scarce. Rapa Nui and its inhabitants suffered greatly after discovery by the Dutch. American and European sealers, whalers, soldiers, and diplomats exploited the people and brought misery and disease to the island. Few natives survived to pass on their people's legends and history.

Theories far outnumbered facts. Some enthusiasts determined that Rapa Nui was once the seat of a brilliant civilization, the vestige of a submerged continent. Others insisted the island was a fabulous lost continent once known as Mu. Rapa Nui, others believed, was a link between the ancient civilizations of Central and South America. The few examples of hieroglyphs found on Rapa Nui— several tablets carved with as yet undecipherable characters—struck some people as similar to script from the Indus Valley. The correspondences inspired them to theorize that the culture of Easter Island was linked to that of Asia or prehistoric China. In his book, *Return to the Stars,* Erich Von Däniken postulated that extraterrestrials had transported the moai from the volcanic cones in which they were carved to their altars by the sea.

Archaeologists quickly debunked many of the early hypotheses. No space aliens carved or moved the monoliths. Easter Island was not a sunken civilization like the fabled Atlantis. But many mysteries remained: Who were the people who created the statues, and why had they worked so hard to carve, move, and erect them, only to topple them centuries later?

RAPA NUI IS A 62-SQUARE-MILE TRIANGLE. IT FORMED WHEN THREE VOLCANOES erupted from the seafloor of the Pacific; their lava flows merged and created the land. The peaks of the cones anchor the three corners of Easter Island. Poike, at

REEDS AND GRASS QUILT A LAKE IN THE CRATER OF RANO KAU,
ONE OF THREE VOLCANOES THAT ERUPTED FROM THE SEAFLOOR
TO FORM RAPA NUI. ONCE A MAIN WATER SUPPLY, THE FRESHWATER LAKE
NOW SUPPORTS CROPS OF AVOCADOES, ORANGES, AND BANANAS.

the eastern end, erupted about 2.5 million years ago and is the oldest of the formative volcanoes. A shallow and dry crater called Puakatiki lies at its 1,214-foot summit. The 1,063-foot-high cone of Rano Kau lies at the southwestern tip of the island. The caldera holds a freshwater lake nearly a mile in diameter. Maunga Terevaka, 1,663 feet above sea level, anchors the northern section of Rapa Nui. Southeast of the larger volcano, a satellite cone, Rano Raraku, rises 490 feet above a nearly flat plain. Its crater, the birthplace of most of Easter Island's stone figures, is composed of tuff, a rock of hardened ash and other fine bits of volcanic debris fused together by heat. Its composition makes tuff soft and easy to sculpt.

Most of the more than 880 statues documented to date on Easter Island were chiseled from tuff; only about 50 were carved of other materials. These hundreds of moai honored island gods and chiefs. About half of them lie in the vicinity of Rano Raraku, the quarry in which they were produced; 396 statues in various stages of completion remain in the crater's quarries.

Most of the other moai were transported and erected on ceremonial structures called *ahu.* Open-air sanctuaries, the ahu were rectangular stone platforms on

which priests and chiefs performed rituals. Ceremonial platforms and statues are found throughout Polynesia, and heads are usually the most important attributes of Polynesian images. However, nowhere are the statues as large or as numerous as on Rapa Nui. Some 270 moai once stood on various ahu scattered throughout the island. They reflect a fundamental Polynesian concern with genealogy and status. Spaced about half a mile apart, each ahu belonged to a particular family group. Most statues were erected along the coast and faced inland, toward the planted fields that sustained Rapa Nui's inhabitants.

The first statues were probably erected soon after the island was settled. The earliest statue known to be mounted on an ahu stands 16 feet tall and is located on the west side of the island. It dates from about A.D. 700. But the islanders erected these statues for centuries. The biggest building boom lasted from 1400 to 1600. In general, earlier moai were smaller than those produced later: The statues gradually increased in size. The smallest statue recorded is about 3 feet tall, and the largest is about 32 feet tall, weighing 89 tons. The average Easter Island moai— that stony sentinel that has come to symbolize Rapa Nui—is 13.3 feet tall and weighs about 14 tons, a manageable rectangle that could be successfully transported and erected.

The Rapa Nui ahu vary in their architecture, but the statues are strikingly similar in shape and design. All the moai associated with ahu are big-headed rectangles, with an elongated head that makes up one-third to one-half of the statue, no matter what its height. All gaze forward. At the waist, the arms reach across the abdomen, and the fingers meet at a central point in the design. All have elongated ears, prominent noses, and pursed lips.

Some of the moai—perhaps 50 to 75 of them—once wore cylindrical hatlike blocks of stone called *pukao*. Some think the pukao represented hats, others that they symbolized hair or bark-cloth turbans. Some experts believe that whatever these topknots were, they served to distinguish the lineage of particular statues. All the pukao were carved from a red volcanic stone called scoria, quarried in Puna Pau, a cinder cone on the western part of Rapa Nui. Throughout Polynesia, the color of scoria—the dark red of dried blood—is held sacred.

The ancient craftsmen fitted some of the moai with indented eye sockets. Most experts believe a statue's eyes were added after the figure was positioned. The pupil

ON HIS SECOND VOYAGE, BRITISH CAPT. JAMES COOK ANCHORED
AT EASTER ISLAND IN MARCH 1774. WILLIAM HOLL II BASED HIS ENGRAVING
OF COOK ON A PAINTING BY NATHANAEL DANCE.

was crafted from red scoria, and the cornea was shaped out of white coral found on the island's rocky coast. Only two sites on Rapa Nui, Anakana on the north coast and Vinapu on the south, have as yet yielded fragments of the white of the statues' eyes, and archaeologists hypothesize that they were probably added to the moai only at special ceremonies held at specific important sites. The people of Rapa Nui believed that the eyes gave the stone statues *mana*, or supernatural power.

ONLY THE RESIDENTS OF EASTER ISLAND SAW THE SENTINELS AS THEY ORIGINALLY stood. By the time Europeans reached the island, the moai were blind and bareheaded, toppled from their platforms, their heads pillowed in grass and dirt. Since then, some have been restored and re-erected. At Tongariki, on the southern coast, 15 of the gray monoliths have been reassembled and returned to their original position in a single row. Archaeologists consider the site one of the greatest religious monuments of early Polynesian culture in the South Pacific. Finely sculpted moai at Ahu Nau Nau have also been re-erected, their red topknots put back in place. Seven bareheaded statues at Ahu Akivi, one of the few inland ceremonial platforms on the island, were restored in 1960. The resurrected moai seem regal and stoic, their spare and graceful outlines reflective of their important place in the world of Rapa Nui.

The statues were commemorative icons, probably representing chiefs, ancestors, or other individuals of high rank. They portrayed leaders who were also regarded as gods in Polynesian culture. Each moai was commissioned by the head of a different lineage on the island or by the son of one of those chiefs. The gods of the people of Rapa Nui manifested themselves to believers in many ways and forms, and the moai were central to the ancestral worship of the island. As in other parts of Polynesia, experts believe each statue represented an empty vessel, a universal male form. Rituals were performed to

summon various gods and deified spirits of revered chiefs into the statues. The moai gave body to these beings and contained mana. Variations among the ahu and the statues themselves suggest that the more powerful gods required more elaborate ceremonial settings. A religious aristocracy ruled Rapa Nui. Its

MYSTERIES OF THE ANCIENT WORLD

ROOSTERS CARVED IN LAVA ROCK TAKE SHAPE AS WALTER AND ANN MARIE KOCH
TRACE THEM WITH TALCUM POWDER AND WATER TO STUDY AND PHOTOGRAPH THEM.
FOUNDING SETTLERS BROUGHT CHICKENS TO RAPA NUI IN THEIR SEAGOING CANOES;
THE ANIMALS REPRESENTED A PRIME FOOD SOURCE FOR ANCIENT ISLANDERS.

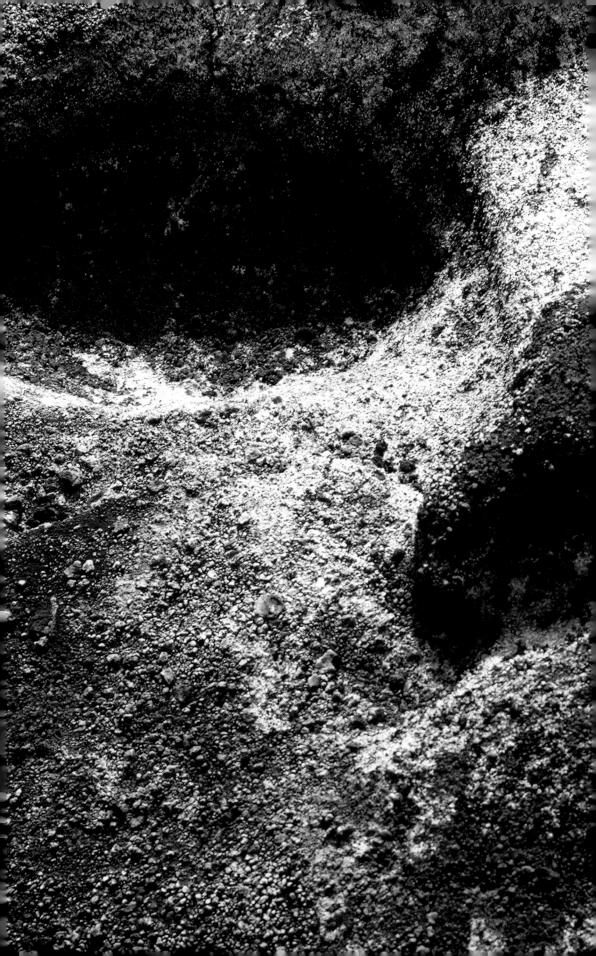

PRECEDING PAGES: MAMMOTH OVAL EYES AND A BROAD NOSE DOMINATE THE FACES OF

RAPA NUI'S MOAI. THE SOFT AND SCULPTABLE TUFF OF THE STATUES, REDDISH ORANGE

WHEN FIRST QUARRIED, WEATHERS OVER TIME TO SHADES OF GRAY, BROWN, AND BLACK.

powerful chiefs could enlist the large labor force necessary to create, move, and erect the huge statues.

Throughout Polynesia, powerful chiefs engaged experts to produce objects of spiritual or social importance—items such as a sacred canoe or a moai. In any Polynesian profession, an expert was known as a *tufunga*. Craftsmen who were very skilled possessed the mana held in such high regard by their culture. The production of a statue was sacred labor. Omens, offerings, and rituals composed of chants, incantations, sacrifices, and prayers accompanied the creation of each statue. The chiefs provided payment in food to the craftsmen, especially delicacies such as lobsters, eels, and tuna, and the statue became the property of the person who had commissioned it and of those of his lineage.

On Rapa Nui the carvers of the moai were called *maori*. The high degree of standardization among their statues suggests that they were well organized and controlled their work carefully. Variations in technical skill as shown in differ-ent carvings lead experts to believe that some of the statues may have been worked by apprentices honing their craft. It appears that Polynesian stone carvers, who elonged to guilds, passed their skills, tools, and rituals on from father to son.

The maori of Rapa Nui chiseled slabs of rock from the crater at Rano Raraku. The island's quarrying methods were similar to those used elsewhere in the Pacific region to cut coral and stone slabs. First, workers roughed out a rectangular slab from the tuff. Then other laborers, who stood in trenches surrounding the block, undercut it. The maori carved a moai as it lay on its side, using adzes or axlike tools made of basalt. Archaeologists have unearthed hundreds of heavy basalt tools from nearly every part of the quarries at Rano Raraku.

Because heads were such an important element of Polynesian images, the carvers may have finished facial features before other attributes, such as hands, were fash-ioned. When the maori had completed their carving, and before the statue was polished, it was moved from Rano Raraku to an ahu over roads built for that pur-pose. The routes, tracks of compacted soil between 9 and 13 feet wide, still wind through the island.

Archaeologists have documented 47 statues abandoned along the roads, and these present one of the biggest unsolved mysteries of Rapa Nui. Most of the moai rest on their backs, but some lie on their faces or sides. The varying positions of

ANCIENT CRAFTSMEN OF RAPA NUI CARVED WOOD AS WELL AS STONE, AND PRESENT-DAY RESIDENTS HAVE REVIVED THE ART. FIGURINES LIKE THE *MOKO*, OR LIZARD MAN, TOP, OFTEN ADORNED THE ENTRANCES TO HOUSES. A CHISELED OVAL MAY REPRESENT A BEETLE OR A SEA SLUG. PEOPLE OF RANK WORE TWO-HEADED *REI MIROS*, OR PECTORAL ORNAMENTS. SHORT-HANDLED IMPLEMENTS POUNDED FOOD.

the statues suggest that they were being moved in different ways. Those lying on their backs were probably being transported horizontally, securely tied to frameworks. Some of the abandoned statues seem to have once stood up. Were those moai that were being transported upright? Or had they been erected along the road as a ceremonial entrance to Rano Raraku? Did they fall while being moved or were they intentionally destroyed? And, finally, why were the statues abandoned? Did something happen to the chiefs who had commissioned them? Were some of the statues just too big to move?

IN 1987 JO ANNE VAN TILBURG, DIRECTOR OF THE ROCK ART ARCHIVE AT THE Cotsen Institute of the University of California, Los Angeles, began studying how the moai were transported. Some experts thought the people of Rapa Nui had moved the statues by rocking them back and forth as they pulled them forward

with ropes, much as one person might rock a piece of furniture across a floor. Others thought the movers placed a moai in a Y-shaped frame of tree trunks and dragged it over rollers of logs. Still others postulated that a moai was swung from spot to spot on a rope suspended from a log derrick until it reached its final resting place. Van Tilburg was convinced that to move the moai, the people of Rapa Nui applied the maritime technology for which the Polynesians were famous.

Polynesian seafarers shared generations of experience in navigation and canoe construction. They were adept in the use of the fulcrum and lever; they knew how to manufacture rope and how to lash it efficiently. Van Tilburg compiled measurements and sketches of various moai to determine the average size and weight of those that were successfully moved to and erected on ahu around the island. Using data from skeletons, she used statistical analysis and computer imaging to calculate that the average Easter Island man was five feet, six inches tall. From that finding, she determined how much force he could exert.

In April of 1998 Van Tilburg and her team built a nine-ton concrete replica of a typical moai and an ahu. Then they set about moving their statue along the original roads from Rano Raraku to its resting site on the coast of the island. Using traditional Polynesian techniques, the researchers constructed a V-shaped sledge similar in design to the double-hulled voyaging canoes of the Pacific seafarers.

At first the team pulled the replica, lashed headfirst on the sledge, across a track of greased logs. When the rollers jammed, they lashed them together and pulled the statue over the track. That method, sliding the stone monolith rather than rolling it, proved more effective. Then the researchers decided to rerig the sledge and move their replica across the island using another Polynesian maritime technique—the canoe ladder.

To haul one of their large seafaring canoes up a slope or over rocks, Polynesians relied on a rope ladder laced with logs as rungs. Islanders slid the vessel over the logs to its destination. In three easy pulls, the researchers moved their concrete moai 150 feet over the lubricated 10-foot rungs of their canoe ladder to the top of a ramp built over the ahu platform. Positioning the moai took nearly a day, and the team piled rocks and dirt below the sledge to raise the statue. Hoisting the sledge, the group then easily levered the moai into place. Van Tilburg's experiment

MINIATURE MOAI: MODERN CRAFTSMEN SHAPE SOUVENIRS CARVED OF PUMICE SIMILAR TO THE VOLCANIC ROCK OF THEIR GIANT COUNTERPARTS. THE KEEPSAKES BRING TOURIST DOLLARS, VITAL TO THE ISLAND'S ECONOMY.

proved that 40 people could pull an average-size moai one mile a day; 20 people could raise a moai, even one wearing a pukao. The team concluded that a Rapa Nui chief and his extended family, using the maritime expertise common among the Polynesians, were easily capable of making, moving, and erecting an average-size moai. Transporting larger statues demanded more people, more time, and more resources. Rapa Nui chiefs achieved only a 10 percent success rate in moving heavier moai.

The sailing skills and epic voyages of the Polynesians are legendary. Originally from Southeast Asia, they reached Tahiti and the Marquesas Islands by A.D. 300 and then sailed to Hawaii and New Zealand. Their navigational skills and marine technology enabled them to explore and settle every habitable island in the world's largest ocean. In huge seagoing rafts and *vaka,* double-hulled canoes one hundred feet long, they traveled thousands of miles, guided by the stars. No one knows why they ranged so widely. Overcrowding may have inspired their voyages. They may have been testing or enjoying their skills and technology, or perhaps younger sons of chiefs sought new lands to rule.

Linguistic, cultural, and genetic evidence has convinced most anthropologists that Rapa Nui was settled by seafaring Polynesians. DNA from 12 island skeletons was tested in 1994, and the results proved that they were the remains of Polynesians. Artifacts unearthed from Rapa Nui are Polynesian in style. Most likely, based on language relationships, Polynesian voyagers sailed from the atoll of Mangareva or the Marquesas, arriving at Easter Island between A.D. 400 and 750. To reach that destination, the Polynesians had to paddle some 2,000 miles against prevailing winds and currents, straying far east and south of their usual routes. The settlers had to locate a scrap of land in the middle of a blue nowhere. Experts believe such an accomplishment could not have been entirely accidental.

DONATED BY A JAPANESE COMPANY, A HUGE CRANE HOISTS A TOPPLED MOAI TO ITS RESTORED PLATFORM DURING THE RECONSTRUCTION OF AHU TONGARIKI BY CHILEAN ARCHAEOLOGIST CLAUDIO CRISTINO BETWEEN 1992 AND 1996.

In 1999 a team of Hawaiians from the Polynesian Voyaging Society—a group that had executed previous expeditions to prove that the Polynesians had the skills for purposeful exploration of the Pacific—set out from Mangareva to duplicate this voyage of settlement to Easter Island. Using only navigational techniques known to the ancient Polynesians, they sailed 1,450 miles to reach their goal. They landed on Easter Island in 19 days. Some experts dismiss their voyage. Their 62-foot twin-hulled Polynesian canoe, *Hokule'a*, was rigged with racing sails and used other modern materials. Detractors argue that it had capabilities far beyond those of any ancient craft.

According to Rapa Nui traditions, however, its settlers did indeed come from the west in canoes. Their ancestral chief, Hotu Matu'a, the Great Parent, sailed east from a land called Hiva, bringing his wife, family, and extended family, and arriving about A.D. 400. He brought crops for planting as well as poultry, and he landed on a beach named Anakena on the north side of the island. Hotu Matu'a divided the land among his six sons. Each son founded a separate family group; each group established its own name and territory. Hotu Matu'a, the progenitor of the next 56 generations of local kings, was considered to be the descendant of Easter Island's supreme god, Makemake, the creator of humankind.

The settlers called their island Te-Pito-o-te-Henua, the navel of the world. Soon after arriving, they explored, divided the territory, and began to establish the crops they had carried with them. Rapa Nui was forested then, but gradually the trees were cleared and the island slopes were planted with bananas, sugarcane, and taro. The bark of paper mulberry trees was used as cloth.

The inhabitants of the island, who lived in cave shelters and houses they constructed of stone, were mainly farmers and fishermen. In traditional Polynesian fashion, the original settlers divided the land into *kaingas*—pie-shaped wedges that extended inland toward the center of the island and outward from the coast into the Pacific. People of an extended family lived communally on hereditary land. The society of Rapa Nui, as on many Polynesian islands, was an aristocratic one divided into an upper class and a working class. The highest-ranking kin group on Rapa Nui, which claimed direct descent from Hotu Matu'a, was the Miru, or Ko Tu'u Aro Ko Te Mata, whose territory was the western part of the island. More numerous, the lower-ranked Hotu Iti Ko Te Mata Iti resided in the eastern part of the island.

As in all tribal societies, organization was based on kin relationships. Patrilineal descent determined a person's group membership, and group determined social status. Each kin group was further divided into classes by occupation: priest, warrior, craftsman, farmer, and fisherman. The highest

ranking person in each group was the *ariki,* or priest. Over all the priests presided the *ariki henua,* whose power was religious rather than political and passed from father to son.

It is likely that one of the first acts of the settlers was the construction of a sacred site. Radiocarbon dating indicates that Ahu Tahai 1, on the western coast of the island, was in use by about A.D. 600. The society and culture of Rapa Nui seems to have evolved in isolation; no evidence exists of any two-way communication with other peoples or places. Anthropologists and archaeologists agree that the monolithic statue cult unique to the island developed during this period. They do not know, however, how and why it emerged and took its particular form on Rapa Nui. The forests that covered the island were cut down to establish farm fields and, perhaps, to use as rollers to transport the moai.

BY ABOUT A.D. 1000, THE POPULATION OF THE ISLAND WAS INCREASING. At the same time, the environment was changing. Rano Raraku and Rano Kau were largely deforested. Quarries at Rano Raraku were in full production, and Rano Kau grew in importance as a ceremonial site. During this phase of Easter Island culture, the scale, size, complexity, and architectural variety of the ahu and cleared ceremonial spaces throughout the island increased and intensified. Anthropologists believe Rapa Nui's population peaked at between 7,000 and 9,000 inhabitants by about A.D. 1550. More and larger statues were produced. Deforestation continued. Although food sources at first increased, the growing population and the increase in moai building put stresses on the island.

Environmental and resource crises inspired the growth of another religion—the Birdman Cult. The arrival of migratory birds from June to August and their nesting in September or October afforded the islanders a valuable seasonal food source. Makemake, the universal creator god of the islanders, became incarnate in a birdman called *tangata manu.* Rituals moved from the ahu sites to Orongo, on the volcanic cone of Rano Kau, where archaeologists have found numerous petroglyphs of the round-faced, goggle-eyed creator deity. Large communal fields were abandoned; the inhabitants of the island survived from the produce of small household

COCONUT PALMS STRETCH TO A WHITE SAND BEACH AT ANAKENA.
ACCORDING TO TRADITION, HOTU MATU'A—THE LEGENDARY FOUNDER OF EASTER
ISLAND—LANDED HERE. LIKE MOST MOAI, THOSE AT AHU NAU NAU FACE INLAND.

gardens. Moai carving came to an abrupt halt in the late 1600s. Incomplete statues were abandoned in the quarries at Rano Raraku, and others were left on lower slopes and along roadways.

Crop failures, perhaps due to drought, produced yet more discontent and stress among the islanders, and varying degrees of conflict developed. Two opposing confederacies of related lineage groups evolved; the lower-ranking clans rebelled against the religious elite. The warring tribes toppled moai, decapitating many of them. Ritual cannibalism, the ultimate insult to the losers by the victors, was long a part of the island culture, but

TWILIGHT SILHOUETTES THE PROUD PROFILES OF MOAI AT AHU NAU NAU.

THEIR PUKAOS MAY REPRESENT HATS, WRAPPED HAIR, CROWNS, OR CLOTH TURBANS

AND MAY HAVE DENOTED A PARTICULAR LINEAGE OR STATUS ON RAPA NUI.

human bones unearthed in trash heaps on Rapa Nui suggest that famine may have forced some inhabitants to resort to cannibalism to survive.

Rapa Nui was struggling in the throes of these crises when sighted by Jacob Roggeveen on Easter Sunday, 1722. His landing interrupted and changed the island culture forever. The three Dutch ships anchored overnight, and the next day more than a hundred armed sailors landed on the shores of the island. Amid the tumult that accompanied their arrival, at least ten inhabitants were killed by the musket-carrying Dutch.

When Roggeveen resumed his voyage, the world learned of a strange Pacific Island populated with colossal statues made of, as he reported, clay. The tremendous impact of the Dutch encounter lasted to 1770, when a Spanish expedition dropped anchor. With great pomp and ceremony, including a parade of priests and soldiers decked out in full regalia, the sailors claimed the island. Four years later British explorer Capt. James Cook, on his second global voyage, visited for five days.

None of the European visitors described how the statues were used in rituals. Roggeveen wrote in his journal only that the inhabitants lit fires before some of their giant statues, then sat before them with heads bowed. Cook noted the existence of the moai, and his account of them helped to make them famous, but neither he nor any other observer recorded seeing a priest conduct a ritual before one of the statues. Cook, furthermore, discouraged other navigators from stopping at the island. "Here is no safe anchorage; no wood for fuel; nor any fresh water worth taking on board," he reported. Nevertheless, a French expedition went to Easter Island in 1786, and their stay there did result in an accurate plan of the ahu and moai.

THE 19TH CENTURY MARKED THE BEGINNING OF A DARK AGE FOR RAPA NUI. The crew of the American schooner *Nancy* raided the island to recruit slaves, and as a result the Easter Islanders grew increasingly hostile to any outsiders. In 1816 a Russian scientific expedition was met with a hail of stones, as was another ship in 1825. Whalers and adventurers continued to inflict cruelties.

In 1862 Peruvian slave hunters, in search of labor for the guano mines on their coast—huge deposits of seabird droppings used for fertilizer—began to decimate

MYSTERIES OF THE ANCIENT WORLD

STARING SKYWARD, AN ABANDONED TEN-FOOT MOAI RESTS ABOVE A LAKE IN THE
CRATER OF RANO RARAKU, BIRTHPLACE OF MOST OF EASTER ISLAND'S STATUES.

the island's population. Among the prisoners kidnapped from the island were King Kaimakoi, his sons and daughters, and revered priests and learned men who were the keepers of the island's ancient culture. One thousand residents were captured; more than nine hundred died within several months from brutal treatment and disease. The bishop of Tahiti interceded with the Peruvian government, and the survivors were returned to their island. Only 15 survived the voyage. The rest died of smallpox, which, when introduced by the repatriated slaves, ravaged Rapa Nui. The island population plummeted to just 111.

In 1864, when Belgian lay brother Eugène Eyraud became the first European missionary to minister to the residents of the island, not a single moai remained standing. In his nine months on Rapa Nui, Eyraud found hungry people dwelling in caves, barely surviving amid social anarchy. By 1877 only about a hundred islanders remained alive.

By 1888, when the Chilean government annexed the island, there was little left of the people or their culture. Their traditions and history survived only in reports of early visitors, folklore, and oral genealogies. The only written records were tablets inscribed with mysterious hieroglyphs first reported by missionaries. Most experts now agree that the symbols, called *rongorongo,* were probably created to serve as reminders of island rituals and date from 1770, when the Spanish annexed the island. The small group of priests and elders from Rapa Nui who could read the characters carved in the 25 or so wooden tablets died as slaves in Peru. The symbols have defied interpretation for decades and remain indeciperable. The script, similar to but in some ways radically different from other Polynesian languages, reminds scholars that the culture of Easter Island evolved over centuries of isolation.

English anthropologist Katherine Routledge was among the first to mourn the knowledge that died with the Rapa Nui elders. Born to a wealthy Quaker family, Routledge was one of the first female graduates of Oxford University. At the then-advanced age of 40, she married Australian adventurer William Scoursby Routledge. Together they built a 90-foot yacht and sailed for the Pacific to mount an expedition to Rapa Nui.

They arrived in March 1914, and Katherine Routledge began the first archaeological survey of the island. In her nearly 17 months there, she mapped the quarries at Rano Raraku, describing how the statues were cut from the rock and precisely locating maoi. The first person to notice that some of them had been forcefully broken, she postulated that some of the statues had once stood upright and had formed a ceremonial entanceway to the crater.

STONE HOUSES AT ORONGO, ON THE RIM OF THE VOLCANO RANO KAU, SHELTERED PARTICIPANTS IN THE BIRDMAN CULT RITES THAT CELEBRATED THE YEARLY ARRIVAL AND NESTING OF THE SOOTY TERN, INCARNATION OF THE CREATOR GOD MAKEMAKE.

French anthropologist Alfred Métraux visited Rapa Nui in 1934, and firmly established that the giant statues of the island had been erected by the ancestors of its residents rather than by members of a mystical lost race. He collected and transcribed the legends, migration myths, and genealogies of the remaining Rapa Nui people. They were familiar, Métraux recognized, with the great Polynesian gods and heroes. Starting with that realization, he suggested that the most important god of Rapa Nui—the creator, Makemake—was the equivalent of the eastern Polynesian god Tane, the first man. According to the legends of eastern Polynesia, Tane erected wooden posts, called sky proppers, to hold the male sky and the female earth apart so that life could develop.

Roggeveen, Cook, and other early visitors to Rapa Nui had recognized the similarities of the island's culture, people, and language to others encountered on other islands of Polynesia. Routledge and Métraux went a step beyond those who preceded them. They not only appreciated the common elements noted before, but they also used the better documented cultures of eastern Polynesian islands, such

EVEN AFTER DECADES OF STUDY, SYMBOLS ENGRAVED ON A WOODEN
RONGORONGO TABLET STILL MYSTIFY EXPERTS. THE EASTER ISLAND GLYPHS
MAY STAND FOR SOUNDS OR KEY IDEAS THAT PROMPTED
STORYTELLERS WHILE RECITING LEGENDS OR GENEALOGIES.

as Mangareva, the Marquesas, and the Tuamotus, to evaluate and study Easter
Island and its culture.

Norwegian explorer Thor Heyerdahl was convinced that the settlers of
Easter Island had come from South America rather than Polynesia. In proof of his
theory Heyerdahl noted the importance of the sweet potato as a staple on Rapa
Nui. Experts agree that it is a South American cultigen. How then, Heyerdahl
asked, did sweet potatoes get to Easter Island, unless they were brought by South
American settlers? The prevailing trade winds, which blow east to west, would have
favored a migration from South America, Heyerdahl insisted.

Intent on proving his hypothesis, he commissioned a 45-foot balsa raft named
*Kon-Tiki* and sailed from Callao, Peru, in 1947. His 5,000-mile voyage to the Raroia
atoll took 101 days; Heyerdahl described the journey in a book that captivated the
world's reading public. He proved that a voyage of settlement from South

America to Easter Island was possible. How the sweet potato made the transition from South America to Polynesia remains one of the great mysteries of this ancient culture.

Although present-day anthropologists dismiss his South American settlement hypothesis, Heyerdahl did contribute to the reservoir of knowledge about Easter Island. In the 1950s he led the Norwegian Archaeological Expedition to Rapa Nui, where his team studied soil levels and layers for the first time. Based on other research, Heyerdahl estimated that six men working full-time every day would need 12 to 15 months to carve a single moai.

IN THE YEARS FOLLOWING HEYERDAHL'S POPULARITY, STUDIES CONTINUED TO shed light on the culture of Rapa Nui. Before his death in 1969, Catholic priest Father Sebastian Englert completed a survey of the stone ahu around the island. Archaeologist William Mulloy and his team restored the seven moai and their ahu at Akivi. In 1978 archaeologist Sergio Rapu, then governor of Easter Island, discovered and reconstructed the coral pieces that comprised the eyes of some of the statues. Chilean archaeologist Claudio Cristino directed the restoration of 15 moai at Tongariki, and by 1996 the statues, heads reattached, somberly surveyed their former domain.

Jo Anne Van Tilburg has been researching the moai and culture of Rapa Nui for more than 20 years. When she arrived, 600 statues had been documented. Now some 880 statues have been located, described, and entered into the database of the Easter Island Statue Project, which she heads. The moai, Van Tilburg believes, elevated the sky from the Earth, allowing light to enter and make the land fertile. As Métraux suggested more than 70 years ago, the statues were props to hold up the heavens. They were closely related to agricultural production, and their size symbolically increased space, ensuring greater fertility and food. As the needs of the islanders increased, so did the size of the moai.

Some experts attribute the decline of Easter Island to its statue cult: To create larger and larger moai, the people of Rapa Nui wasted more and more of their limited resources, until they finally self-destructed. Van Tilburg interprets their history differently. We may never know exactly what the statues meant in the lives of the people of Easter Island; we may never understand what drove them to create such images of power and presence; we may never fully appreciate how interrelated events brought the demise of their culture. Despite those questions, for Van Tilburg, as for many others, the moai of Rapa Nui stand as mute testimony to the cultural achievement—not failure—of a people who dared to claim as their own one tiny corner of the wide Pacific.

# Motherhood to Moai Maven

Jo Anne Van Tilburg has studied the moai of Rapa Nui for more than two decades and is the world's leading expert on the statues. Her journey to that status was serendipitous.

Born in Minneapolis in 1942, Van Tilburg graduated from the University of Minnesota with a bachelor of science degree in 1965 and began teaching in a California junior high school. In 1968 she married architect Johannes Van Tilburg. Their daughter, Marieka, was born in 1974. After ten years of teaching, Van Tilburg decided to quit and devote herself to the career of mother and homemaker.

By the time Marieka reached preschool, however, Van Tilburg was growing restless. When another preschool mother invited her to help with an archaeological dig underway at a nearby building site, Van Tilburg accepted. The archaeologist in charge happened to take his workers to a Chumash Indian site to view their pictographs. For Van Tilburg: "It was a turning point in my life."

She returned to college to study archaeology. In 1982 her interest in rock art took her to Easter Island, where a colleague was studying rock carvings. "The petroglyphs were interesting," she recalls, "but I fell in love with the statues." Van Tilburg determined to find and catalog each moai—then thought to number about 600—on the island. She has completed seasonal fieldwork on Rapa Nui ever since. In 1986 she earned her Ph.D. degree in archaeology from the University of California, Los Angeles, and in 1989 she received a grant from the National Geographic Society.

The Easter Island Statue Project, of which she is the director, has thus far measured, mapped, and cataloged 887 moai on 210 sites throughout Rapa Nui and estimates some hundred sites remain to be surveyed. "On the island," remarks Van Tilburg, "archaeology is on the surface. It's so visible, so audacious."

Van Tilburg has applied a technical approach in learning about the island and its moai. With the help of a computer, she used data from skeletons to find the average size of an early Easter Island man—he was about 24 years old, five and a half feet tall, and weighed 150 pounds—then calculated how much force he could have applied to moving a statue.

Careful measurements, cluster research, and computer modeling revealed that the average moai weighed 14 tons. Gathering all this information, Van Tilburg factored in statue size, terrain, and the force necessary to move a moai. She concluded that it would take 63 people about 30 hours to transport a typical statue some ten miles from its quarry to its ahu, or ceremonial base. Raising the moai, she calculated, would likely take another 30 hours.

Previous scientists had suggested how the statues may have been transported, but no one had actually tried to move one. Van Tilburg and her team were the first when, in 1998, they rolled a concrete replica from the crater of Rano Raraku to the coast of Rapa Nui.

ROPE WRAPS A MOAI AS ARCHAEOLOGIST JO ANNE VAN TILBURG PREPARES TO MEASURE AND PHOTOGRAPH IT. SHE AND HER TEAM HAVE MAPPED NEARLY A THOUSAND EASTER ISLAND STATUES.

Van Tilburg credits much of the success of the Easter Island Statue Project to the people and agencies of Rapa Nui. With their cooperation, she says, archaeology is a "valuable bridge between the past, present, and future." The computerized database of the project will never be closed; new discoveries will be entered, and Van Tilburg will continue to be part of the effort: "I think that, if I hadn't found Easter Island, what began as an avocational interest in archaeology might not have developed into an intellectual and professional challenge, and then into a personal quest," Van Tilburg has commented. "I did, and it has, and I feel very, very lucky."

# CHAPTER 6

## Africa's City of Stone

### GREAT ZIMBABWE

LARGEST SINGLE PREHISTORIC STRUCTURE SOUTH OF THE SAHARA, ZIMBABWE'S GREAT ENCLOSURE CONTAINS AN ESTIMATED ONE MILLION BRICKS STACKED IN LAYERS TO FORM WALLS UP TO 32 FEET HIGH.

# Chapter Six

**LARGEST AND MOST SPECTACULAR**
ruins south of the Sahara, the mortarless walls of Great Zimbabwe
sprawl across some 1,800 acres of wooded plain in the remote
southeastern highlands of Zimbabwe. These ruins inspired the
name of that African nation. Great Zimbabwe, once the capital of
an inland kingdom rich in cattle and gold, is one of some 300
known stone enclosure sites on the Zimbabwe Plateau; it is by far the
largest and most complex. The powerful chieftains of Zimbabwe ruled
a rich medieval kingdom known to Islamic traders along the entire
length of the east African coast. Like many ancient sites, it has been
shrouded in legend and wrapped in mystery since its discovery by
Europeans more than a century ago. The white adventurers who stumbled
on the ruins near the end of the 19th century long claimed nonliterate
Africans could never have built such a settlement. The ruins were variously
attributed to the Phoenicians, Arabs, or Romans. Some people determined
that the site was the golden city of Ophir mentioned in the Bible. Others

insisted that it was Axuma, one of the cities of the fabled Queen of Sheba. Yet another theory postulated that Great Zimbabwe was the creation of Prester John, legendary Christian king of all lands beyond the Islamic realm. For decades white explorers, exploiters of the continent's vast natural resources, and colonists of the nation that was originally called Rhodesia refused to accept the city's African origin. Although their racist biases finally fell to archaeological reality, some genuine puzzles still baffle experts. Why did its founders choose the highlands for their huge settlement? Why did the city finally fall?

MANY EXPERTS BELIEVE THAT GREAT ZIMBABWE WAS AN EARLY CAPITAL OF the Shona people that evolved into an important medieval trading city. Some interpret the word "Zimbabwe" as a contraction of a Shona phrase meaning "houses of stone." Others translate the phrase as "venerated houses." It is the millions of stones of the ruins—squared and tightly fitted without mortar—that distinguish the massive site between the Zambezi and Limpopo Rivers some 200 miles due south of the present capital city of Harare. Archaeological data indicate that the houses were indeed "venerated"—they were chiefs' dwellings or graves.

The settlement of Mapungubwe, some 140 miles southwest of Great Zimbabwe, predated the walling techniques, architectural vision, and sophisticated stonework of the capital. Mapungubwe thrived for some 200 years, reaching its height in about A.D. 1250; by 1290 Great Zimbabwe had eclipsed it. Some archaeological evidence indicates that iron was in use at the site by the third century A.D. Many archaeologists and anthropologists believe that bands of Shona cattle herders, attracted by the mild climate and open grasslands of the Zimbabwe Plateau, had settled there by A.D. 500. The altitude—3,000 to 5,000 feet above sea level—offered respite from the tsetse flies that plagued herds grazing at lower elevations. The southeastern plains offered abundant grazing, fertile fields, timber, and proximity to gold and salt mines.

Great Zimbabwe lay on a route between Africa's gold-producing regions and ports such as Sofala on the coast of present-day Mozambique. The inhabitants of Great Zimbabwe traded gold dust from the Limpopo River, packed in porcupine quills, along with iron tools, copper ingots, rhinoceros horns, and elephant tusks. In return, they received glass beads, fabric, and porcelain from lands abutting the Indian Ocean. Increased contact with Arab merchants along the eastern coast during the ninth and tenth centuries brought prosperity to the growing city.

**AT THE HEART OF GREAT ZIMBABWE RISES THE CONICAL TOWER,
ITS PURPOSE STILL A MYSTERY. THE RUINS OF THE MEDIEVAL CITY EVOKE ITS
HEYDAY AS A CAPITAL OF THE SHONA PEOPLE IN THE 14TH AND 15TH CENTURIES.**

By 1250 Great Zimbabwe had become one of several major cities on the Zimbabwe Plateau. Its scale compared to other sites in the area suggests its political and economic importance. Trade mushroomed. Persian faience bowls, coral, bronze bells, Syrian glass beads, and celadon dishes from China's Ming dynasty have all been unearthed at the site. These artifacts prove that Great Zimbabwe was a well-established trading center by the 14th century.

During its heyday, from the 14th to the 15th centuries, as many as 18,000 people lived in Great Zimbabwe, Africa's largest precolonial city. Its inhabitants, the Shona people, believed that the city's chiefs transcended the boundaries between the spiritual and material worlds and were the intermediaries between the living and their revered ancestors—the *adzimu*. These chiefs ruled as the dominant political force on the plateau, thus controlling much of interior southeastern Africa for some two centuries.

CONSTRUCTED BETWEEN ABOUT A.D. 1100 AND 1500, GREAT ZIMBABWE IS UNUSUAL for its stonework as well as its size. Ancient masons raised walls more than 30 feet high using no mortar. Instead they used a method called the dry-stone technique, finding or cutting rocks to fit and laying them down with nothing to cement them together. The builders found their stone in the bare granite hill that backs the site. The rock split easily along fracture planes into roughly rectangular shapes and therefore lent itself to dry-wall stacking. None of the slabs interlock; all were set in layers to form stable, freestanding walls. They range in thickness from 4 to 17 feet and are about twice as high as they are wide. Some of the finest that remain are as smooth as modern baked brick.

Great Zimbabwe contains three distinct areas: the Hill Complex, the Great Enclosure, and the Valley Complex. The Hill Complex, built into the 62-foot-high granite dome that overlooks the rest of the site, was the most sacred part of Great Zimbabwe. Chiefs and their priests made intercessions for rain here and performed ancestor rituals. Sometimes called the "Acropolis" by Europeans, it is the oldest part of Great Zimbabwe, dating to about 1250. An outer wall nearly 37 feet high surrounds an oval enclosure some 328 feet long and 148 feet wide. The stone wall merges with high granite boulders of the rocky hill on which it is built. On its western edge lies another enclosure some experts think may have contained residences of chiefs or the privileged elite.

Below the Hill Complex lies the most impressive of the site's stone structures—the Great Enclosure. It is the largest single prehistoric structure south of the Sahara and contains an estimated one million granite blocks, more stone than in all the site's other ruins combined. An 800-foot-long elliptical outer wall, 32 feet high in places and with three narrow entrances, surrounds the enclosure.

An inner wall runs along part of the huge outer wall, creating a cramped and narrow passage 180 feet long that dead-ends at the most mysterious building in Great Zimbabwe—a flat-topped conical tower 30 feet tall. This

GOLDEN SUNLIGHT CASTS THE SHADOW OF A PALM TREE ON THE ROCKS
OF THE RUINS. MASONS QUARRIED LOCAL GRANITE, WHICH FRACTURED EASILY
INTO ROUGH RECTANGLES, TO BUILD THE CITY BETWEEN A.D. 1100 AND 1500.

beehive-shaped structure, 18 feet in diameter at its base, is built around a solid core and lacks stairways or rooms. According to Shona traditions, tributes of grain were stored in large clay bins at other chiefs' enclosures. Perhaps the Conical Tower performed a symbolic function in Great Zimbabwe: It may have represented the chief's ability to feed his people.

The inner part of the Great Enclosure dates to the early 14th century, when Great Zimbabwe was at the height of its power. Construction of the outer wall began about a century later. Experts do not know the function of the Great Enclosure. It may have served as a royal palace, or it may have housed the ruler's many wives. Residents living at the site when Europeans found it in the 19th century called the Great Enclosure *Imbahuru*—the house of the great women, or the great house.

A smaller series of compounds in the valley between the Hill Complex and the Great Enclosure, the Valley Complex was built in the early 15th century. It was probably constructed as the population of Great Zimbabwe grew and the city needed more residential space. The mortarless walls of the settlement that stand today were only part of the city. They were the skeleton that protected the many dwellings that lay within them—little of which remain. The residents of the city used *daga*—dried earth, mud, and gravel—to raise their curved, hut-like houses. The mixture, plastic and easily shaped when wet, is still the most common indigenous building material throughout Africa.

Few traces of the red mud homes—more susceptible to rain and weather than granite—remain. European treasure hunters and explorers destroyed many of the buildings in their clumsy attempts to excavate Great Zimbabwe. Vegetation and rubble hide most of the partial structures that remain, but their close relationship to architecture throughout the continent is clear proof of the African authorship of the site. The sophisticated stonework of the standing walls reveals the skill and power of a people at their peak.

AFTER 300 YEARS OF SUPREMACY IN THE SOUTHEAST, HOWEVER, GREAT ZIMBABWE began to decline. As the population of the city increased, farming and grazing may have depleted the soils; salt probably became scarce. The number of inhabitants of Great Zimbabwe dwindled. By the mid-15th century the balance of trade began to shift.

With the fall of Great Zimbabwe, two Shona states rose to dominate the gold-rich plateau territory. In the south, Butua, or Torwa, rose to prominence. The kingdom of Mutapa flourished in the north, near the Zambezi River. By 1500 its dynasty ruled a large part of the territory and tried to control the critical trade routes to the coast. Great Zimbabwe remained largely empty for some two centuries, used occasionally for religious ceremonies. Portuguese missionaries and explorers who arrived on the southeast African coast shortly after the fall of Great Zimbabwe were the first to hear and relay rumors of the city of stone to the south.

Reports began reaching the coastal trading ports of Mozambique in the 16th century. Portuguese chronicler João de Barros described "a square fortress, masonry within and without, built of stones of marvelous size, and there appears to be no mortar joining them." Lured by whispered descriptions and visions of gold, Europeans began searching for the stone ruins. The earliest European records of the city were made by a young German geologist, Carl Mauch, in 1871. Seeking the legendary city of Ophir, in August Mauch reached the home of a local hunter named Adam Render, who told him of "quite large ruins, which could never have been built by blacks." The European refusal to accept African origins for Great Zimbabwe began.

On September 5, Karanga-speaking tribesmen—Karanga is one of the most common dialects of the Shona language—led Mauch to the stone walls of Great Zimbabwe. Its Karanga inhabitants knew little of its archaeological history. The mysteries deepened, and theories proliferated. Mauch, who noted what he thought was a cedar lintel in one of the walls, determined that the wood must have come from Lebanon, brought by Phoenicians. Great Zimbabwe, he insisted, had been built by the Queen of Sheba. Years later the lintel proved to be made of African sandalwood, a local hardwood also used in the construction of the walls of the Great Enclosure.

German hunters Harry and Willi Posselt followed on the heels of Mauch. The Karanga protested in vain as Willi Posselt hacked a soapstone bird from its base along one ruined wall of the Eastern Enclosure, then used as a cattle pen, and hid three others for later looting. The desecration of Great Zimbabwe began early and continued unabated for years. The soapstone carvings, unique to Great Zimbabwe, would come to represent the heritage of a nation.

Financier and investor Cecil Rhodes founded the British South Africa Company to profit from the natural resources of the African continent during its period of European colonization. Rhodes bought Willi Posselt's Great Zimbabwe bird and, interested to learn more about the ancient site, sent archaeologist James Theodore Bent to explore the city. Although all the artifacts he unearthed—among them spearheads, axes, and gold-working equipment—were obviously of indigenous origin, Bent tenaciously clung to the idea that Great Zimbabwe was non-African in origin. A prehistoric "northern race

CURVING STONEWORK OF THE OUTER WALL OF THE GREAT ENCLOSURE, AT LEFT,

AND A SECONDARY INNER WALL CREATE THE PARALLEL PASSAGE, A CRAMPED AND

NARROW CORRIDOR 180 FEET LONG THAT ENDS AT THE CONICAL TOWER.

coming from Arabia" built the city, he insisted. Digging around the Conical Tower, Bent destroyed the soil layers, threw away clay and metal artifacts, and thoroughly corrupted the site. He found the three soapstone birds that Posselt had tucked away and discovered yet another, together with half of a second bird, in the same enclosure.

Appointed curator of Great Zimbabwe by Rhodes in 1902, journalist Richard Nicklin Hall scoured it for evidence of its white builders. He discarded archaeological deposits throughout the site, leaving only vestiges for future study. Most of the daga houses were destroyed, creating erosion problems that persist today. He found and removed another Great Zimbabwe bird and the upper half of another.

W. G. Neal, commissioned by Rhodes to exploit the ruins of the country—by then named Rhodesia, after him—contributed more damage to Great Zimbabwe along with many other areas, looting them of gold and everything else of value, razing structures, and trashing artifacts such as pots and figures that he considered useless. Like Bent, Neal and Hall subscribed to the attitude pervasive in colonialist Africa: Great Zimbabwe was Phoenician or Arabic; the black tribes of Africa could not have developed such a site.

IN 1905 EGYPTOLOGIST DAVID RANDALL-MacIVER WAS THE FIRST LEGITIMATE excavator to visit Great Zimbabwe. Unlike previous visitors, he turned to the indigenous Karanga and Shona peoples for clues about Zimbabwe. Based on the continuity of artifacts found as well as the curved stonework of the walls, Randall-MacIver concluded that native Africans had built Great Zimbabwe some six centuries earlier. The city, he proclaimed, was "unquestionably African in every detail." His pronouncement outraged the settlers of Rhodesia, the hue and cry so great that no further excavations were made at the site for more than two decades. From 1914 to 1931 St. Clare Williams, curator of the ruins, conducted a restoration. But his misguided and inaccurate work, based, like that of his predecessors, on the tenet that the city was non-African, further sullied the site.

It was not until 1929 that archaeological excavations resumed at Great Zimbabwe. Englishwoman Gertrude Caton-Thompson arrived at the site in an oxcart. She, like Randall-MacIver, focused on the site's architecture and small artifacts. "There was," she found, "not a single item that was not of African origin and medieval date." Roger Summers examined the ruin in 1955, studying soil layers to determine its age. Summers and two other investigators, Keith Robinson and Anthony Whitty, began digging in 1958. Using the newly available method of radiocarbon dating, they estimated the age of Great Zimbabwe accurately for the first time. Thomas Huffman, in the 1970s, honed their data. Even the careful and scientific excavations of these archaeologists left scars on the site. Wooden structural supports were removed to perform the radiocarbon dating.

Based on the results of those tests, archaeologists believe that the first inhabitants, cattle herders and farmers, arrived at Great Zimbabwe in about A.D. 300. We may never determine who they were. They did not settle, and perhaps they only grazed their herds where the ruins now lie. For the next four centuries Great Zimbabwe was deserted while Shona groups elsewhere built up large herds of cattle. Some of those groups had settled at Great Zimbabwe by the seventh or eighth century. To our knowledge, they built no stone walls, but their strong traditions of ancestor worship contributed to the site's growth as a revered shrine and center for rain ceremonies. Stone monoliths and altarlike structures among the ruins hint at its importance as a religious center. One of the mysteries of Great Zimbabwe is how it grew so rapidly. Within a few centuries, it developed into a sizeable and prosperous kingdom. Given the scale of the city, archaeologists still cannot explain its sudden appearance on the plateau.

MOST OF THE ARCHAEOLOGISTS WHO HAVE STUDIED GREAT ZIMBABWE WERE trained and spent the larger part of their lives outside Africa. Peter S. Garlake, Rhodesia's Senior Inspector of Monuments from 1964 to 1970, was born, raised, and educated in that African country. He brought a different perspective to Great Zimbabwe research, taking into account its local history, traditions, and anthropology.

An expert on the ancient Shona, Garlake noted that ancestor worship was an important part of that culture's religion. He thought the soapstone birds and other figures found in Great Zimbabwe indicated the important role of rituals and symbols in the architecture and art of the site. Most European settlers in Rhodesia, despite growing evidence, rejected the archaeological record. In the 1960s the Rhodesian Front—a party based on the system of apartheid, dedicated to preventing Africans from gaining power in the country, and led by Prime Minister Ian Smith—suppressed the findings of

Garlake and other prehistorians who claimed that Africans had built Great Zimbabwe. Garlake, among others, was imprisoned and later deported.

During the 1960s, as Great Zimbabwe became a major tourist attraction, the Rhodesian Front controlled all access to the site. It was developed with no regard for its cultural significance or history. A museum and even a golf course were built, facilities that destroyed yet more of the archaeological remains. The Rhodesian Front and its control of Great Zimbabwe fueled a reaction called the African Nationalist movement, which adopted the site as a potent political symbol. During the 1960s and 1970s, escalating friction between whites and blacks led to fighting and guerilla warfare in Rhodesia. The United

HEADRESTS, WHICH SUPPORTED THE NECK OR HEAD AND PROTECTED THE OWNER'S ELABORATE COIFFURE AS HE SLEPT, HAVE BEEN USED IN AFRICA FOR CENTURIES. CROSSED SUPPORTS, CHARACTERISTIC OF SHONA HEADRESTS, MAY HAVE REPRESENTED OUTSTRETCHED ARMS AND LEGS.

WEATHERED WALLS AND HOUSE MOUNDS MARK A RESIDENTIAL AREA OUTSIDE THE
GREAT ENCLOSURE, MEAGER REMAINS OF A CITY OF UP TO 18,000 PEOPLE.

African National Council came into power, and the country became the independent nation of Zimbabwe in 1980, the only nation in the world named after an ancient monument.

RESEARCH CONTINUED AFTER INDEPENDENCE. SOME OF IT CENTERED ON HOW Great Zimbabwe developed into such an influential power. The abundant grasslands of the area could assure ample grazing, but the soil is poor and would not have supported the farming necessary to supply the city's growing population. Experts now recognize that Great Zimbabwe's inhabitants did not begin to exploit the rich gold deposits of the plateau until perhaps a century after the founding of the city.

Thomas N. Huffman, of South Africa's University of Witwatersrand, has studied the plateau's early settlements together with 18 other sites contemporary with Great Zimbabwe. The combination of political and economic power with religion, all vested in the chieftain, Huffman believes, allowed Great Zimbabwe to rise in prominence. In harmony with Garlake, Huffman hypothesizes that the turrets, towers, and soapstone birds of Great Zimbabwe were rife with religious symbolism.

Huffman's research has also convinced him that a great distinction made between males and females at the site was reflected in the city's stonework. Chevron patterns in the walls of the Hill Complex were associated with young men; dark stripes and herringbone patterns in the walls of the Great Enclosure were female signs. The narrow passageways and entrances in various parts of the ruins indicate, according to Huffman, that some areas were reserved for the king and his entourage or other elite individuals. The Eastern Enclosure, from which Willi Posselt stole the soapstone birds, was the most restricted of all areas.

David N. Beach, of the University of Zimbabwe, rejects Huffman's conclusions and suggests that the rise of Great Zimbabwe was more random. Beach believes that the city grew due to the chance appearance of three or four generations of charismatic leaders. Mount Holyoke historian Eugenia Herbert contends that Great Zimbabwe grew due to the mining of nearby metals and the metalworking skills of its inhabitants. The remains of utilitarian and luxury items crafted of iron, copper, gold, and bronze have been found in the ruins. The recent work at Great Zimbabwe reflects a new subscience, cognitive archaeology, in which scholars try to penetrate the ancient human mind. Such an approach may be the best hope to decipher the puzzles of Great Zimbabwe, a nonliterate society that left no written records and a site stripped of nearly all archaeological records by careless excavation and casual exploitation.

**FIST RAISED IN TRIUMPH, ZIMBABWE'S PRESIDENT, ROBERT MUGABE, CELEBRATES THE REUNION OF TWO HALVES OF A SOAPSTONE BIRD. IN 2003 GERMANY RETURNED THE BOTTOM PORTION, STOLEN FROM CITY RUINS IN THE LATE 1800s.**

One of the tragedies of Great Zimbabwe is that so much information and history has been lost due to racist denial; another is that politics and racial bias still haunt the site and impede research. Political violence in Zimbabwe and attacks initiated by its president, Robert Mugabe, on whites in the country have driven visitors from the great stone city. Tourism, which was once such a vital industry, has all but vanished, and the economy of the nation of Zimbabwe seems to be approaching collapse.

ABOVE: SHONA MOTHER AND CHILD BALANCE BUNDLES. THE SHONA TODAY
NUMBER ABOUT NINE MILLION. MANY LIVE NEAR THE RUINS OF THE ANCIENT CITY.
OPPOSITE: THE HILL COMPLEX, OLDEST PART OF GREAT ZIMBABWE, OVERLOOKS THE
REST OF THE RUINS. THE SUNLIT WESTERN ENCLOSURE HOUSED THE ELITE;
PRIESTS CONDUCTED RITUALS IN THE SHADOWED EASTERN ENCLOSURE.

Great Zimbabwe has survived many decades of European interlopers, desecration, and prejudice, and yet the ancient city—its site and its mysteries—continues to beckon. What were the great chiefs like—the men who mobilized the workforce to raise such a citadel in so short a time? What religious beliefs shaped the design of the city? Many tribes lay claim to the site; did the ancient Shona build it? Why was it finally abandoned?

In 1931 Gertrude Caton-Thompson declared: "The mystery of Zimbabwe is the mystery which lies in the still pulsating heart of native Africa." Her words still ring true. The stone walls of Great Zimbabwe solidly evoke the presence of a successful civilization—a city with a population equivalent to that of medieval London—in the midst of the land once called the "Dark Continent."

# EMBLEMS OF A NATION

Great Zimbabwe's soapstone birds have intrigued archaeologists since German hunter Willi Posselt first chopped one from a wall of the Eastern Enclosure of the Hill Complex in 1889.

Within a few years, a total of eight of these statues were found in the ruins. They are unique—the only sculptures from Great Zimbabwe, or any other prehistoric site in south-central Africa of any complexity and size, that demonstrate an attempt at stylized, symbolic representation.

All are carved from soft, dark, green-gray soapstone. They stand about 14 inches high, and originally they topped columns about three feet tall. The birds were sculpted by whittling away excess stone, a carving process that suggests that their sculptors were experienced at working with wood.

Although the birds have been variously identified as eagles, hawks, vultures, and even parrots, their creators made no attempt to depict specific species. The carvings are symbolic icons, but archaeologists do not know—and probably never will—what exactly they represented. Because contemporary Shona hold their dead in high regard, some archaeologists believe the statues symbolized revered ancestors and were used in rituals.

A different pattern or marking sets each bird apart, but all of the statues share common characteristics. The creatures sit rather than perch, their legs plump and rounded, gripping with four or five human-like toes rather than talons. Their beaks are crude extensions of the heads instead of differentiated parts of the body. The wings look like bony plates, and incised parallel lines on the surfaces of some are the only indications of plumage.

Five of the birds squat solidly on bent legs. Their heads jut forward at 90-degree angles to their necks. Their wings come to a point in the back of the sculptures, and they have no tails. These five avians were carved on top of rectangular columns with narrow fronts and long sides; each form flowed smoothly into its base. The column of one of these is ornately carved with the figure of a crocodile as well as circular and chevron motifs, designs that can be found in the stonework of the outer wall of the Elliptical Building as well.

Limp legs hang down from the bodies of two other birds and from the bottom half of a third. Each of these birds grasps a molding and has squarish wings and a short, fan-shaped tail. All gaze slightly upward, their elongated vertical forms similar in shape to the cylindrically shaped plinths they adorn. One of these birds is characterized by incised lips instead of a fully formed beak.

Despite the protests of the local Karanga inhabitants, who held Great Zimbabwe sacred and were determined to protect the relics, the soapstone birds were stolen from the ruins. First Posselt absconded with one. Then James Theodore Bent found the three that Posselt had hidden and two others. Richard Nicklin Hall made off with one bird and part of another. Cecil Rhodes, who bought Posselt's stolen bird, displayed it at his official residence—

FOUND BY ARCHAEOLOGIST JAMES THEODORE BENT IN 1891, THIS SOAPSTONE BIRD TOPS A COLUMN FROM GREAT ZIMBABWE'S EASTERN ENCLOSURE.

Groote Schuur, in Cape Town, South Africa. The lower half of one bird somehow found its way—probably stolen even before Bent's visit—to the Museum für Völkerkunde—the Ethnological Museum—in Berlin, Germany. A head retrieved by Hall in the Western Enclosure was later found to fit this piece perfectly.

In 2003 Germany returned that carving to Zimbabwe. In all, seven birds have returned home. Ironically, the only bird missing is the first one stolen, removed by Willi Posselt in 1889 and sold to Cecil Rhodes as he exploited the resources of the African continent.

Icons of an ancient people, the soapstone birds of Great Zimbabwe have become emblems of a modern nation. Their shape adorns the country's flag, bank notes, and currency. Like the ruins, they have become a symbol of Zimbabwe's proud past.

# About the Author

Toni Eugene is the author of 25 books. She was on the staff of the National Geographic Society's Book Division for more than 20 years before relocating to Charlotte, North Carolina, in 1992. Since then she has been a freelance editor and writer for various organizations. For the Society, she most recently wrote *Mystery of the Ancient Seafarers: Early Maritime Civilizations* with Robert D. Ballard and edited the *National Geographic Encyclopedia of Space*.

# Additional Reading

Paul G. Bahn, ed., *Cambridge Illlustrated History of Archaeology* (Cambridge University Press, 1996)

*Builders of the Ancient World: Marvels of Engineering* (National Geographic Books, 2000)

Patricia S. Daniels and Stephen G. Hyslop, *Almanac of World History* (National Geographic Books, 2003)

Brian M. Fagan, *Into the Unknown: Solving Ancient Mysteries* (National Geographic Books, 1997)

*Mysteries of Mankind: Earth's Unexplained Landmarks* (National Geographic, 1992)

*Mysteries of the Ancient World* (National Geographic Books, 1979)

*Peoples and Places of the Past: The Illustrated Cultural Atlas of the Ancient World* (National Geographic Books, 1983)

Maurizio Forte, *Virtual Archaeology* (Harry N. Abrams, 1997)

*Wonders of the Ancient World: National Geographic Atlas of Archaeology* (National Geographic Books, 1999)

*Wonders of the World* (National Geographic Books, 1998)

## On Stonehenge:
Aubrey Burl, *The Stone Circles of Britain, Ireland, and Brittany* (Yale University Press, 2000)

Christopher Chippindale, *Stonehenge Complete* (Thames and Hudson, 1994; 3rd edition, 2004)

## On Native American Mounds:
Ron Fisher, *America A.D. 1000: The Land and the Legends* (National Geographic Books, 1999)

George Milner, *The Moundbuilders: Ancient Peoples of Eastern North America* (Thames and Hudson, 2004)

Robert Silverberg, *Mound Builders of Ancient America: The Archaeology of a Myth* (New York Graphic Society, 1968; reissued, Ohio University Press, 1986)

George E. Stuart, *Ancient Pioneers: The First Americans* (National Geographic, 2003)

George E. Stuart, "Who Were the 'Mound Builders'?," NATIONAL GEOGRAPHIC, December 1972

## On the Standing Soldiers of Xi'an:
*China's Buried Kingdoms* (Time-Life Books, 1993)

Peter Hessler, *Rising to Life* (National Geographic Books, 2001)

Erling Hoh, "China's Great Enigma," *Archaeology,* September/October 2001

O. Louis Mazzatenta, "China's Warriors Rise from the Earth," NATIONAL GEOGRAPHIC, October 1996

O. Louis Mazzatenta, "Chinese Emperor's Army for Eternity," NATIONAL GEOGRAPHIC, August 1992

Audrey Topping, "China's Incredible Find," NATIONAL GEOGRAPHIC, April 1978

## On the Nasca Lines of Peru:
Anthony F. Aveni, *Between the Lines: The Mystery of the Giant Ground Drawings of Ancient Peru* (University of Texas Press, 2000)

John B. Carlson, "America's Ancient Skywatchers," NATIONAL GEOGRAPHIC, March 1990

Loren McIntyre, "Mystery of the Ancient Nazca Lines," NATIONAL GEOGRAPHIC, May 1975

Evan Hadingham, *Lines to the Mountain Gods: Nazca and the Mysteries of Peru* (University of Oklahoma Press, 1988)

Tony Morrison, *Pathways to the Gods: The Mystery of the Andes Lines* (Harper & Row, 1978; Academy of Chicago Publishers, 1988)

## On the Moai of Easter Island:
Richard Conniff, "Easter Island Unveiled," NATIONAL GEOGRAPHIC, March 1993

Thor Heyerdahl, *Easter Island: The Mystery Solved* (Random House, 1989)

Howard La Fay, "Easter Island and Its Mysterious Monuments," NATIONAL GEOGRAPHIC, January 1962

André Metraux, *Easter Island: A Stone Age Civilization of the Pacific* (Oxford University Press, 1957)

Mrs. Scoresby Routledge, "The Mystery of Easter Island," NATIONAL GEOGRAPHIC, December 1921

Jo Anne Van Tilburg, *Easter Island: Archaeology, Ecology, and Culture* (Smithsonian Books, 1995)

Jo Anne Van Tilburg and Ted Ralston, "Engineers of Easter Island," *Archaeology,* November/December 1999

## On Great Zimbabwe:
Robert Blake, *A History of Rhodesia* (Alfred A. Knopf, 1978)

Peter S. Garlake, *Great Zimbabwe* (Stein & Day, 1973)

Roderick J. McIntosh, "Riddle of Great Zimbabwe," *Archaeology,* July/August 1998

Ndoro, "Great Zimbabwe," *Scientific American,* November 1997

Wilfrid Mallows, *The Mystery of the Great Zimbabwe: A New Solution* (W. W. Norton, 1984)

Sean Sheehan, *Cultures of the World: Zimbabwe* (Marshall Cavendish, 1993, 1996; Benchmark Books, 2004)

# Index

Adena people: culture 56; culture decline 59; Hopewell and 59; mounds, burial 56; origin 59; stone tablets 57; territory 56

African Nationalist movement 177

Ahu Nau Nau moai, Easter Island **128-129**, 138, **153**, **154**, 155

Ahu Tongariki moai, Easter Island **130**, 132, 137-138, **148**

Ahu Vai Uri moai, Easter Island **144-145**, 146

Ancient world, definition 8

Arthur, King 46

Astronomy: Ring of Brogar, Scotland 20; megaliths 20-21; Nasca lines, Peru 105, 107-110; Nasca lines, Peru orientation and 121, 122; Standing Stones of Callanish, Scotland 20; Stonehenge, England and 40, 42-43

Aubrey Holes 30, 43

Aubrey, John 30, 36, 40

Avebury, England: as ritual site 16; sarsens **22-23**, 24

Aveni, Anthony F. 110-111, 114-115

Biomorphs 97-100, 110

Blake, William **38**, 39

Breaker People Mass Grave, Wiltshire, England **35**

Ring of Brogar, Scotland **18-19**, 20, **28-29**; erection date 29; height 19; as lunar observatory 20; Thom's study of 20

Cahokia, Ill., U.S. 66; Monks Mound 66; Mound 72 66

Cahuachi, Peru 122; as Nasca religious center/shrine 104; radiocarbon dating 105; Silverman's study of 104-105

cannibalism 153-155

Castlerigg Stone Circle, England **32-33**, 34

Chillicothe, Ohio, U.S. 56

Conus Mound, Ohio, U.S. 62

Cook, James **137**, 155

Craig Mound, Okla., U.S. 66-67

Cresap, W. Va., U.S. 56

Davis, Edwin Hamilton 68-69

Dolmens **26**

Druids **36-37**, 40

Earthwatch exercise 101

Earthworks 69; geometric 69; Hopewell 59-62; Mississippian Period 63; Newark, Ohio, U.S. **48-49**

Easter Island (Rapa Nui) 128-163, 133-147 see also Moai, Easter Island; Rapa Nui people; Ahu Nau Nau moai **128-129**, **153**, **154**, 155; Ahu Tongariki moai **130**, 132, 137-138, **148**; Ahu Vai Uri moai **144-145**, 146; Chilean annexing of 158; Cook's expedition to **137**, 155; environmental/resource crisis 152; foreign expeditions to 155, 158; glyphs 132, **138-139**, **160**; Heyerdahl's expedition to 160-161; land division 149; location **10**, 131; Maunga Terevaka 133; Métraux's expedition to 159, 161; Poike 132-133; Polynesian culture on 138, 147-148, 159-160; population peak 152; Rano Kau 133; Rano Raraku moai **150-151**, 152; religious aristocracy rule of 138, 142; Routledge's expedition to 158-160; settling of 148-149; slaves taken from 155, 158; smallpox plague 158; South American settlers on 160-161; Spanish claim of 155; sweet potato on 160-161; volcanoes 132-133; western discovery of 155; wood carvings **143**

Easter Island Statue Project 162-163

Effigy Mound culture 63

Egyptologists 8

Etowah, Ga., U.S. 67

Ft. Hill mound, Ohio, U.S. 62-63

Geoffrey of Monmouth 46-47

Geoglyphs: biomorph 97-100; campos barridos 100; creating 101; geometric form 96-97; Nasca lines, Peru 92-127; types 96-97

Grand Menhir Brisé, Brittany, France 24

Grave Creek Mound, W. Va., U.S. 56-57

Great Enclosure, Great Zimbabwe, Africa **164-165**,

**166,** 168; construction 170, 172; function 172; granite blocks in 170-172; no mortar in 168; residential area outside **178-179;** walls, outer/inner **174,** 175

Great Serpent Mounds, Ohio, U.S. **50,** 52; mapping 68; origin 63

The Great Wall of China 74, **80,** 81

Great Zimbabwe, Africa **164-165,** 164-185; African Nationalist movement adoption of 180; African origin 167, 173, 175, 183; as capitol of Shona people 168; Conical Tower **169,** 172; construction 170, 180-181; decline 172-173; desecration 173, 175, 177; distinct areas 170-172; Eastern Enclosure **182,** 183, 184; European records of 173; excavations 172, 175, 176; granite use in 170, **171;** Great Enclosure **166,** 168, 170-172, **174,** 175; growth 176; Hill Complex 170; housing material 172; Huffman's study of 180; location **10,** 168; looting 175, 185; male/female distinction in 180; mining 180; mortar use 168; as political symbol 180; political/economical importance of 169; population 170; racism and acceptance of 183; radiocarbon dating 176; Randall-MacIver's excavation of 175; random construction of 180; restoration 175; Rhodes and 173, 175, 185; as Rhodesia 175; Rhodesian Front control of 177-180; soapstone birds 173, 175, **181,** 184-185, **185;** stonework 172; tourism 177, 183; trade in 168-169, 172; Valley Complex 170, 172; Western Enclosure **182,** 183

Heyerdahl, Thor 160-161

*History of the Kings of Britain* (Monmouth) 46

Hopewell ceremonial center, Ohio, U.S. 59-62

Hopewell Culture National Historical Park, Ohio, U.S. **64-65,** 66

Hopewell people: Adena decline and 59; burial mounds 59; burial objects/goods 59; ceremonial blade 66, **67;** culture decline 63; earthworks 59-62; excavation/ mounds of 59;

Ft. Hill mound, Ohio, U.S. 62-63; Seip mound, Ohio, U.S. 62; trade practices **58,** 66; Woodland Period 59

Huffman, Thomas N. 180

Kolomoki, Ga., U.S. 63

Kosok, Paul 107-110, 126

looting: Great Zimbabwe, Africa 175, 185; Mount Li, China 84, 85; Soapstone birds, Great Zimbabwe, Africa 175, 181, 184-185

Maeshowe, Scotland 17-18

Maunga Terevaka, Easter Island 133

Maya people 10-11 *see also* Temple of Inscriptions, Palenque, Mexico

Megalithic yard 21-24

Megaliths: astronomy and 20-21; Avebury, England 16; Ring of Brogar, Scotland **18-19,** 20; Bronze Age 16; Maeshowe, Scotland 17, 20; Neolithic Age 16; Newgrange, Ireland 16-17; Standing Stones of Callanish, Scotland 16, 20; Stonehenge, England 16

Merlin 46-47

Métraux, Alfred 159, 161

*Milton* (Blake) **38,** 39

Minoan Palace, Phaistos, Crete 9-10 *see also* Phaistos Disk

Minos, Palace of, Knossos, Crete 9

Mississippians: Cahokia, Ill., U.S. 66; chiefdoms 66; culture decline 67; earthworks 63; mounds **57,** 66-67; Temple Mound Period of 63-66; Woodland Period 63

Moai, Easter Island 131; abandoned **156-157;** Ahu Nau Nau **128-129, 153, 154,** 155; Ahu Tongariki **130,** 132, 137-138, **148;** Ahu Vai Uri **144-145,** 146; carving process 142; color 136, 137; as commemorative icons 138; commission of 138, 142; craftsmen 142; erection 133-136; eye sockets 136-137; family group 136; features 136-137, **140-141,** 142; formation 132-133; genealogy/status and 136; halt, carving of 153; hatlike blocks on 136, **154,** 155; material 133, 142; platforms, ceremonial 133-136; radiocarbon dating 152; Rano Raraku **150-151**, 152; re-erection 137-138; replication experiment 161, 163; replications/souvenirs **147**; restoration 137-138, 146, **148**, 161; shape/design 136; significance, spiritual/social of 142; size 136; theories 132; transportation 142-147, 163; transportation replication 146; Van Tilburg's study of 143-147, 161, 162-163, **163**

Monemutensis, Galfridus *see* Geoffrey of Monmouth

Monks Mound, U.S. **60-61,** 62

Monoliths: Carnac, France **26**; Grand Menhir Brisé, Brittany, France 24

Mound City, Miss., U.S. 62, 68

Mounds, North America 48-69; Adena 56; Archaic Period 53; building collapse 52; burial, conical 69; Cahokia, Ill., U.S. 66; Chillicothe, Ohio, U.S. 56; construction 53; Conus Mound, Ohio, U.S. 62; Craig Mound, Okla., U.S. 66-67; Cresap, W. Va., U.S. 56; Effigy Mound culture 63; Etowah, Ga., U.S. 67; excavation destruction 62-63; flat-topped temple, pyramidical 69; Ft. Hill mound, Ohio, U.S. 62-63; geometric designs 52; Grave Creek Mound, W. Va., U.S. 56-57; Great Serpent Mounds, Ohio, U.S. **50**, 52, 63; Hopewell 59, 62; Hopewell ceremonial center, Ohio, U.S. 59-62; Kolomoki, Ga., U.S. 63; locations **10**, 51-52; mapping 68-69; Mississippian **57**, 63-66; Monks Mound, U.S. **60-61**, 62; Mound City, Miss., U.S. 62; Moundville, Ala., U.S. 67; National Military Cemetery, Vicksburg, Miss., U.S. **54-55,** 56; Ohio River Valley, U.S. 52; origins 51; platform 63; Poverty Point, La., U.S. 53-56; radiocarbon dating 53; Robbins Mounds, Ky., U.S. 56; Seip, Ohio, U.S. 62; shell ring 52; Swift Creek, Ga., U.S. 63; Thomas's study of 52-53; trade indicators in 56; Watson Brake, La., U.S. 53; Woodland Period 56

Moundville, Ala., U.S. 67

Mount Li, China 70-91 *see also* Qin Shi Huang Di; Xian soldiers, Mount Li, China; artifact preservation 88-89; booby-traps 75; bronzes 78; burial mounds near 88; craftsmen skill 78-81; excavation 88; looting 84, 85; mercury levels 85, 89; non-military statues near 88, **89**; plan 74-75; riches 75; terraced pit 74; tourism 73; underground palace 74; walls 78

Myrddin *see* Merlin

Nasca people 95; Cahuachi in 104-105, 122; ceramics 102, 104, **106**, 107, **124**; colors **115**; culture 102, 104; decline 102, 104; development level 102; field site 165 121-122; funerary 104; habitation sites 104; human heads, mummified and 104; Inca and 114; irrigation channel construction by 102; motifs 102, **111**; nature and 102-104; plague 102; radiocarbon dating and 105; Spanish Conquest 102; spiritual life 118-119; weaving 102

Nasca lines, Peru **92-93,** 92-127; aerial view **123**; animals represented by 104; astrology and 122-125; astronomical orientation 121, 123; astronomical purpose of 105, 107-110; Aveni's study of 110-118; biomorph 97-100, **98-99**; bird 100, 119; campos barridos 100; climate and 95, 100-101, 123; construction methods 101-102; creating 101; damaged 100, 121-122; Earthwatch exercise 101; geometric form 96-97; Hummingbird **112-113,** 114; as irrigation system 107; Kosok's study of 107-110, 126; location 96; main area 96; mapping 104-105; measuring/mapping of 97; Needle and Loom 100; Owl Man **94**, 96, **98-99**, 100; Pan American Highway and **92-93,** 125; political unit creation/maintenance of 121; purpose of 105; radial centers 114-115; Reiche's study of **97**, 110, **116-117**, 118, 126-127; Reinhard's study of 118-119; as ritual pathways 105; rock borders 101; scientific exploration of 107; Silverman's study of 104-105, 121; size 96; solar alignments 110-114; Spider **108-109**, 110, **120**, 121; spiritual life of Nasca and 118; spokelike patterns 111, 114; symmetry 110; themes 119-121; threats 125; time periods 121; tourism 110; types 96-97; visibility **103**; water and 118-119, 125; water sources mapped by 122; Xesspe's study of 105-107, 126

Newgrange, Ireland 16-17

Phaistos Disk 9-10 *see also* Minoan Palace, Phaistos, Crete

Poike, Easter Island 132-133

Poverty Point, La., U.S. 53-56

Great Pyramid of Giza, Egypt 8-9

Qin Shi Huang Di, Emperor, China *see* Shi Huang Di, Emperor, China

Racism 181

Radiocarbon dating 42; Cahuachi, Peru 105; Great Zimbabwe, Africa 176; moai 152; mound 53; Nasca culture 105; Stonehenge, England 42

Randall-MacIver, David 175

Rano Kau, Easter Island 133

Rano Raraku moai, Easter Island **150-151**, 152

Rapa Nui *see* Easter Island

Rapa Nui people: Birdman Cult religion 152, **159**; cannibalism 153-155; canoe construction 146; culture 132, 152; culture collapse 161; land division 149; native culture loss 158; population peak 152; religious aristocracy rule 138-142; as slaves 155-158; smallpox plague 158; social structure 149-152; warring tribes 153

*Records of the Historian* (Sima Qian) 84, 90

Reiche, Maria **116-117**, 118, **127**; astronomical theory 110; Kosok's work with 126; Nasca Line measurements/mapping **97**, 110; Parkinson's disease 116-117, 118, 127

Reinhard, Johan 118-119

Rhodes, Cecil 173-175, 185

Rhodesia, Africa 175

Rhodesian Front 177-180

Robbins Mounds, Ky., U.S. 56

Routledge, Katherine 158, 159

Seip mound, Ohio, U.S. 62

Qin Shi Huang Di, Emperor, China 73, **91** *see also* Mount Li; Xian soldiers; assassination attempts 84; death 84; dynasty 74; empire 74; Great Wall of China and 81; immortality sought by 90-91; legends 90-91; people alienated from 84; public works 74; tomb plan 74-75

*Shiji, Records of the Historian see Records of the Historian* (Sima Qian)

Shona **183**; Great Zimbabwe, Africa as capital of 168; headrests **177**; religious rites 183

Silverman, Helaine 104-105, 121

Sima Qian 84, 90; *Records of the Historian* 84, 90; Qin Shi Huang Di tomb described by 75

Soapstone birds, Great Zimbabwe, Africa 173, **185**; characteristics 184-185; looting 175, 181, 185; as political symbol **181**, 185; reconstructed **181**, 185; Rhodes and 185; symbolization 184

Sphinx, Egypt 8

Squier, Ephraim George 68-69, **69**

Standing Stones of Callanish, Scotland 16, 20

Standing Stones of Stennes, Scotland **25**

Stone rings, British Isles **2-3**, 5

Stonehenge, England 12-47, **14**; Altar Stone 27, 40; astronomical theories 40, 42-43; Aubrey Holes 30, 43; bluestone circle 25, 27, 39; bluestone origin 39; bluestone transportation 39; Breton connection to 24; construction 27-40, **34**; Druids and **36-37**, 40; evolution 15; excavation 21, 42; exterior structure 24; graves near 30, **31**; Heel Stone 27; lintel placement 34; lintel ring 39; lintels 24, 25, 27; location **10**; Merlin and **46**, 46-47; *Milton and* **38**, 39; modification 39; as mortuary site 30; mysteries 43; orientation 42; orientation change 30; purpose 42-43; radiocarbon dating 42; remodeling 30; restoration

21; sarsen circle 24, 34, 39; sarsen placement 34-39; sarsen stone shaping 34; sarsen stone source 34; sarsen stone weight 34; Slaughter Stone 27; Station Stones 27; Station Stones erection 30-34; stone origin 24, 25, 27, 34, 39; stone size 27; stone transportation 27, 34, 39; summer solstice celebration **12-13**; symbolic significance 30; tourism **41**, 42; trilithons 27; written records relating to 42

Swift Creek, Ga., U.S. 63

Temple Mound Period, Mississippian 63-66

Temple of Inscriptions, Palenque, Mexico **6**

Terra-Cotta Warriors and Horses Museum, China **70-71**, 81

Thom, Alexander 20-24

Thomas, Cyrus 52-53

Tiger of Qin *see* Qin Shi Huang Di, Emperor, China

Tombs *see also* Dolmens: Ireland 17; Maeshowe, Scotland 17-18; Qin Shi Huang Di, Emperor, China 70-91

tourism: Great Zimbabwe, Africa 177, 183; Mount Li, China 73; Nasca lines, Peru 110; Stonehenge, England **41**, 42

Van Tilburg, Jo Anne **163**; Easter Island Statue Project 162; moai transportation studied by 143-147, 162-163; National Geographic Society Grant 162; statues located and described by 161

Watson Brake, La., U.S. 53

Woodland Period: Hopewell 59; Mississippian 63; mounds 56

Xesspe, Toribio Mejía 105, 107, 126

Xian soldiers, Mount Li, China **1**, **5**, 70-91, **72** *see also* Qin Shi Huang Di, Emperor, China; detail 81, **82-83**, 84; location, geographical **10**; pit architectural plan 81, 84; pits 78, 81, 84; reconstruction 81, **85**; replications **79**, **86-87**, 88; weapons 78

## Photo Credits

# MYSTERIES OF
# THE ANCIENT WORLD

*By Toni Eugene*

*Published by the National Geographic Society*

**John M. Fahey, Jr.,** President and Chief Executive Officer

**Gilbert M. Grosvenor,** Chairman of the Board

**Nina D. Hoffman,** Executive Vice President

*Prepared by the Book Division*

**Kevin Mulroy,** Vice President and Editor-in-Chief

**Marianne R. Koszorus,** Design Director

**Barbara Brownell Grogan,** Executive Editor

*Staff for this Book*

**Susan Tyler Hitchcock,** Project and Text Editor

**John C. Anderson,** Illustrations Editor

**Peggy Archambault,** Art Director

**Victoria Garret Jones,** Researcher

**Dan O'Toole,** Editorial Assistant

**Carl Mehler,** Director of Maps

**Matt Chwastyk,** Map Production

**Greg Ugiansky,** Map Production

**R. Gary Colbert,** Production Director

**Richard S. Wain,** Production Project Manager

**Meredith Wilcox,** Illustrations Assistant

**Robert Swanson,** Indexer

*Manufacturing and Quality Control*

**Christopher A. Liedel,** Chief Financial Officer

**Phillip L. Schlosser,** Managing Director

**John T. Dunn,** Technical Director

**Alan Kerr,** Manager

One of the world's largest nonprofit scientific and educational organizations, the National Geographic Society was founded in 1888 "for the increase and diffusion of geographic knowledge." Fulfilling this mission, the Society educates and inspires millions every day through its magazines, books, television programs, videos, maps and atlases, research grants, the National Geographic Bee, teacher workshops, and innovative classroom materials. The Society is supported through membership dues, charitable gifts, and income from the sale of its educational products. This support is vital to National Geographic's mission to increase global understanding and promote conservation of our planet through exploration, research, and education. For more information, please call 1-800-NGS LINE (647-5463) or write to the following address:

NATIONAL GEOGRAPHIC SOCIETY
1145 17th Street N.W.
Washington, D.C. 20036-4688 U.S.A.
Visit the Society's Web site at
www.nationalgeographic.com.

Library of Congress Cataloging-in-Publication Data

Eugene, Toni.
  Mysteries of the ancient world / by Toni Eugene.
    p. cm.
  Includes bibliographical references and index.
  ISBN 0-7922-3813-3 (hardcover)
  ISBN 0-7922-3814-1 (deluxe)
  1. Civilization, Ancient.  2. Earthworks (Archaeology)
  3. Geoglyphs.  4. Antiquities.  5. Antiquities, Prehistoric.
  I. Title.

  CB311.E84 2005
  930--dc22

                    2004060970